FINDING

YOUR

authentic

SELF

FINDING YOUR *authentic* SELF

More than 200 unique, focused writing
prompts and self-exploration exercises

SUSAN REYNOLDS

chartwell
books

"Authenticity is a collection of choices that we have to make every day. It's about the choice to show up and be real. The choice to let our true selves be seen."

—BRENÉ BROWN

FOREWORD

If you've been curating your life as a series of perfect social media posts, you're probably exhausted. All that perfection comes at a cost—both actual financial costs as well as emotional and health tolls. So how do you stop presenting who you think you should be and start living authentically, as who you really are? How do you live your life according to your own values and goals, rather than those of other people? The answer is not to disengage from media or other people altogether—there's a better way!

That better way is the workbook you now hold in your hands. Through a series of writing exercises over seven chapters, you will learn to:

- *Observe Yourself Objectively*
- *Explore Your Values, Strengths, and Personality*
- *Manage Your Emotions*
- *Develop Compassion*
- *Live with Integrity*
- *Find Your Life Purpose*
- *Live an Authentic, Meaningful Life*

Once you realize your true potential, you won't care what others think because you will be living your own personal truth. With inspiring and uplifting quotes and affirmations to inspire you along the way, you will discover the fulfillment and peace that comes from living as a more authentic person, a more genuine you. Let's begin.

"This above all: to thine own
self be true, and it must follow,
as the night the day, thou canst
not then be false to any man."
—William Shakespeare, *Hamlet*

Contents

INTRODUCTION

We are all born with an authentic, essential self, a part based on our genetics and unique to us. It may include a proclivity for music or math or writing, or an athletic ability, or the kind of brain that works faster and more furiously than others. It may be an emotional capacity that makes you more open and accepting, someone capable of exceptional empathy or the ability to inspire others to action; it may make you more closed off and protective, someone who requires extended periods of silence in which to create masterful works of art.

"The greatest act of courage is to be and to own all of who you are—without apology, without excuses, without masks to cover the truth of who you are." —Debbie Ford, *Courage: Overcoming Fear & Igniting Self-Confidence*

As we grow up, we learn—mostly in response to our initial caregivers—to tailor our personalities and behave in certain ways, some of which suppress or obfuscate our authentic self. If you had devoted, focused caregivers, you may develop an ability to feel safe in most situations, to learn quickly, to love exploring your environment—to grow up as the authentic self that is uniquely *you*. If, however, you had distracted, unstable, punishing, controlling, or even abusive caregivers, you may foster an underdeveloped, even fearful, anxious personality, have difficulty learning or forming relationships, and suppress your authentic self to make yourself more "acceptable." Adopting social behaviors—in response to caregivers, teachers, religious instructors, authority figures, your culture, and even friends—may have the cumulative effect of burying, or at least concealing, your authentic, essential self.

Ideally, we develop patterns of behavior and make choices and decisions based on the interplay of our authentic and our social selves: your authentic self identifies who you are and who you want to be, and your social self does what is required to fulfill your dreams. But, for many, they allow their essential, authentic *self* to fade into the background and rely on their social self to make most decisions.

The more your authentic self is ignored, suppressed, or eventually so buried you don't know how to be *that* person anymore, the more you feel like a helpless, hopeless imposter. Sacrificing your authentic self often leads to a "dark night of the soul," in which you realize you've been spinning your wheels in the wrong direction and must do the work required to reset your inner compass. So, how do you know if you're living your authentic self? It's easier, perhaps, to know when you aren't.

Are You Living Your Authentic Life?

Sometimes it's easier to know when you're not living an authentic life. Here are eight ways to know you're not honoring your essential self:

1. **You're tired.** *When a rigid social self runs the show—and the essential self is being neglected—you may feel lethargic or depressed. Are you in the wrong job? The wrong relationship?*

2. **You're often sick.** *It gets harder and harder for your social self to keep doing what your essence rejects. Burying or ignoring your essence exacts a price.*

3. **You're forgetful.** *If there's something you really don't want to do, forgetting becomes a way to self-sabotage. If this keeps happening, notice what you're avoiding—and why.*

4. **You make a lot of mistakes.** *When your social self is "forcing you" to do something your authentic self finds repulsive, you unconsciously sabotage yourself.*

5. You openly dislike someone. *We are hard-wired to be socially gracious and accepting, but if someone is anathema to what your authentic self requires, you may fake attempts to be polite, solicitous, or accommodating.*

6. You feel caught in fight-or-flight mode. *Remaining in situations that deny your authentic, essential self will cause adrenaline to run high, leading to a pattern of restless days and nights.*

7. You succumb to addiction. *Neglecting your authentic self creates a painful feeling of emptiness, leading you to seek a substance—food, drink, drugs, bad relationships—that temporarily dulls the pain.*

8. Your moods aren't congruent. *Your moods aren't appropriate to whatever situation you're in, thus your social self can no longer control your moods. Pay attention when this happens as it may signal what your authentic self wants.*

> "One's philosophy is not best expressed in words; it is expressed in the choices one makes. In the long run, we shape our lives and we shape ourselves. The process never ends until we die. And the choices we make are ultimately our own responsibility."
>
> —ELEANOR ROOSEVELT

Let's take a small quiz to see where you are.

Can you identify your essential, authentic self—those parts of you that come naturally, who you are when you most feel like *you*, and any gifts or proclivities you may have that make you stand out from others? List them here.

Not really

Can you identify your social self—those parts of you that were either inspired or drilled into you by your family, religion, school, or friends? For example, are you polite even when angry? Are you unfailingly, compulsively thoughtful?

How do your authentic self and your social self vary? Where do they compete? Are you aware now of places in your life where you suppress your authentic self?

Do you act in ways that you feel are required to make you likable? How does this manifest? Do you feel suppressed as a result?

_____

_____

_____

_____

_____

_____

_____

_____

Do you present a false front designed to elevate your social status? For example, are you posting only "perfect" pictures or exciting events on social media? If so, what does this say about your values?

_____

_____

_____

_____

_____

_____

_____

Now that you've taken this brief status quiz, have you identified aspects of your social self that need revision? We'll be working on this throughout the workbook, but if you are clear on what may be holding you back from living *your* authentic life, go ahead and make a preliminary list of social presumptions you've relied on in the past that you would like to change.

1. _____

2. _____

3. _____

4. _____

5. _____

We're going to explore a multitude of ways for you to rediscover, reconnect to, and reignite your essential, authentic self, but, for now, list three ways you can immediately act more from your unique, authentic self.

1. _____

2. _____

3. _____

Now that we've established where you are, let's work on skills you can develop to live more authentically.

HOW TO KNOW WHEN YOU'RE IN ALIGNMENT WITH YOUR AUTHENTIC SELF

Just as there are many signs that you're not living your authentic life, there are obvious indications that you are in alignment:

1. **Your energy level surges.** When you're engaged in doing what you love, what comes naturally and brings you joy, your energy level runs high.
2. **Your health or immune system improves.** When you're authentic, you experience less stress, which bolsters your health.
3. **Your brain lights up.** It focuses better, retaining massive amounts of information about what excites you.
4. **You are in "the flow."** Your creative juices are running, ideas abound, and excitement is high.
5. **You attract positive people** who are supportive, encouraging, and invigorating.
6. **You're often in a great mood.** You feel optimistic and excited about life.

"In *all* circumstances, what you believe determines your actions. Your actions determine your future. The choice of how you live and what becomes of you is in your own hands."

—WU WEI, *I CHING LIFE: BECOMING YOUR AUTHENTIC SELF*

CHAPTER ONE

OBSERVE YOURSELF OBJECTIVELY

If you're like most people, you judge yourself too harshly, worry that you're far less than you should be—or could be. You can probably quickly list a multitude of your faults but would have difficulty listing your strengths, and you likely show yourself little compassion. Who is that internal monitor and why are they so strident? Who are you judging yourself against? Is your life really so unhappy?

To reclaim your authentic self, you have to assess where you are in the present moment.

"Only the truth of who you are, if realized, will set you free."

—ECKHART TOLLE, *A NEW EARTH: AWAKENING TO YOUR LIFE'S PURPOSE*

Where Are You Now?

To see yourself *objectively*, it might help to pretend you are a researcher assigned to write a biography about you. To assess how you're doing so far, in terms of living an authentic life, answer the following queries.

What *most* defines you? List the five most important aspects of your life. Give this some thought before answering.

1. _____
2. _____
3. _____
4. _____
5. _____

What currently rules your life? What would you *like* to rule your life?

_____

_____

_____

_____

Do you generally *like* whom you have become? Why or why not?

_____

_____

_____

Are you in the right profession? Does it suit you? Does it make you happy? Is there something else you've always wanted to do instead?

_____

_____

_____

_____

_____

Have you traveled far from where you began geographically, emotionally, or intellectually? Are you *where* you want to be? Are you living a lifestyle that fulfills you? What would you like to change?

_____

_____

_____

_____

_____

Think about the five most important people in your life. Who offers genuine emotional support? Who matters most to you? Do you make sufficient time for them? Are you genuinely connected to them?

1. _____

2. _____

3. _____

4. _____

5. _____

If you had to write your own eulogy—what makes you most notable and memorable to others—what would be the highlights?

1. _____
2. _____
3. _____
4. _____
5. _____

What's missing that you'd like to have there?

1. _____
2. _____
3. _____

Are you starting to see areas in which you're not living authentically? No need to write about them here, as we'll be working through the process of identifying and addressing them as you progress through this workbook. Now that you have a general picture of where you are, let's zoom in a little tighter.

"We are betrayed by what is false within."

—GEORGE MEREDITH, *MODERN LOVE*

Where's Your Head?

Are you feeling lost? Confused? Discouraged? Cynical? Distrusting? Closed? On the wrong path? We all get stuck in emotional hard places, experiencing days, weeks, months, or even years when we feel lost or confused, heartbroken and discouraged, or short-fused and cynical. Life, in effect, challenges and breaks us repeatedly. We spend months, or years, reassembling ourselves, searching for a positive, upbeat, strong-minded, optimistic grip on life to pull us out of whatever hole we've fallen into.

Before you can grab the lifeline and pull yourself out of that hole you're currently in, you need to see clearly what's pitched you into the darkness. Ponder the following questions, then write about what your particular challenge is.

- *Have you experienced recent disappointment?*
- *A physical challenge?*
- *The loss of a loved one through illness, death, physical separation, a breakup?*
- *Friends pulling back?*
- *A career setback?*
- *Financial devastation?*
- *Overwhelming challenges?*

Now *pinpoint* the source of your current emotional challenge. Be as specific as possible. Be sure to examine your role in creating, or excessively enduring, said mindset.

List three actionable steps you can take to address what's been holding you back.

1. _____
   _____
   _____
   _____

2. _____
   _____
   _____
   _____

3. _____
   _____
   _____
   _____

"Highly sensitive people are too often perceived as weaklings or damaged goods. To feel intensely is not a symptom of weakness, it is the trademark of the truly alive and compassionate."

—ANTHON ST. MAARTEN

Where's Your Heart?

While our heads tend to land us in jeopardy, it's our hearts that ultimately right the ship. Rather than overthinking, we need to *feel* our way out. Sometimes you cannot launch that process until you've unleashed all the pent-up emotions connected to the challenge. Ponder the following questions, then write about your heart challenge.

- *Have you cried all the tears?*
- *Written about the heartbreak?*
- *Absorbed all the sordid details of your story?*
- *Grieved the loss?*

What has been holding you back emotionally? If there's nothing specific at the moment, maybe it's a difficulty identifying, feeling, and expressing your *true* emotions?

_____

_____

_____

_____

_____

_____

_____

_____

_____

What do you *feel* is needed to right your emotional ship?

_____

_____

_____

_____

_____

_____

_____

_____

_____

_____

WRITE IT OUT

Therapy is an effective way to deal with whatever heartache or emotional challenge has landed you in a netherworld of pain and disappointment, but you can begin by writing about what is troubling you most. Be sure to list any steps you can take to jump-start solutions, including seeking outside help.

Where's Your Body?

Our poor bodies often suffer the most. Our mental and emotional challenges manifest in aches and pains, illnesses, and a plentitude of other ongoing physical symptoms that plague our daily life. This is not a frivolous matter: physical pain is often generated by emotional pain.

How would gauge your level of stress? What specifically is causing the stress?

_____

_____

_____

_____

_____

_____

Are you having physical symptoms? If so, where are they located?

_____

_____

_____

_____

_____

_____

What are you doing to address the underlying problem that causes the pain?

_____

_____

_____

_____

_____

_____

_____

How are you treating your body in general? Are you comfortable in your body? If not, why?

_____

_____

_____

_____

_____

_____

_____

"Best keep yourself clean and bright; you are the window through which you see the world."

—GEORGE BERNARD SHAW

Where's Your Soul?

Are you doing anything to honor your soul? Are you religious? Spiritual? Someone who relies on a self-created moral compass? Do you pray, journal, meditate, write poetry, or read self-help books? Maybe you don't do any of those things, but if not, how are you honoring your soul, that deepest part of yourself? Neglecting this aspect of life makes it hard to live authentically.

Do you believe your soul has value? Why?

_____

_____

_____

_____

_____

_____

What are you doing to connect with your innermost thoughts and beliefs?

_____

_____

_____

_____

_____

_____

_____

What can you do to reinforce the parts of your soul that make you *you*?

_____

_____

_____

_____

_____

_____

_____

_____

_____

_____

_____

Now that you have a broad overview of where you currently are in your journey, to bolster your opportunities to live an authentic life, let's find out more about what defines you.

> "Constantly exposing yourself to popular culture and the mass media will ultimately shape your reality in ways that are not necessarily conducive to achieving your Soul Purpose and Life Calling. Modern society has generally 'lost the plot.' Slavishly following its false gods and idols makes no sense in a spiritually aware life."
>
> —ANTHON ST. MAARTEN

CHAPTER TWO

EXPLORE YOUR VALUES, STRENGTHS, AND PERSONALITY

To validate that our truest self has real value, we need insight into our essence. Kira Asatryan, author of *Stop Being Lonely*, suggests that learning to love yourself can prove as futile as trying to convince someone else to love you. However, loving yourself is crucial to reconnecting with your authentic self and finding your life purpose because having deep knowledge of yourself leads to a feeling of closeness and compassion that is, in effect, loving your*self*.

According to Asatryan, feeling close and loving towards yourself is crucial to the ability to find intimacy with another. If you don't know yourself, how will anyone else? Getting closer to your inner self is something you can do on your own, and it often makes you feel happier and more fulfilled. You'll also gain more understanding of your needs and values, as well as more awareness of how to care for yourself, a greater ability to recognize and express your feelings, and more readiness for intimacy with a significant other.

What Do You Like About Yourself?

Often what we find most attractive in others are qualities that we ourselves possess. Are you a hard worker? Devoted to family? Faithful in relationships? Unfailingly honest? Fun-loving? Generous? Passionate about politics? Working hard to save the planet? An adventurer? Creative explorer? Genuinely kind towards others? A dependable volunteer? Someone who pursues her passion? Someone who rescues pets? Someone who responds to texts quickly and attentively?

List ten things you *truly* like about yourself. If you find this daunting, try thinking of what you find most attractive in other people; often, when we really think about it, we possess the very qualities we find desirable in others.

1. _____

2. _____

3. _____

4. _____

5. _____

6. _____

7. _____

8. _____

9. _____

10. _____

What Are Your Strengths?

Strengths are aspects of your personality, intellect, or body that make you stand out from others. These are often considered talents, or natural skills, things that you excel at doing. Or it can be skills you've learned that come easily to you, something that has garnered top grades or accolades. Or it can be your facility with relationships, nurturing children, forming friendships, or working with others in communal action. Or maybe you have a splendid green thumb and actively nurture nature.

What five things are you particularly good at doing?

1. _____

2. _____

3. _____

4. _____

5. _____

What are your *unique* talents (for empathy, art, verbal expression, music, nurturing, teaching, etcetera)?

1. _____

2. _____

3. _____

Are you using them? If not, why?

_____

_____

_____

_____

_____

_____

_____

_____

_____

_____

_____

_____

_____

_____

_____

_____

_____

_____

_____

_____

_____

_____

_____

CONSULT ONLINE

If you have difficulty knowing what your strengths are, online questionnaires such as the Values in Action Inventory or the Clifton Strengths Assessment can be helpful.

What Are Your Weaknesses?

Weaknesses are those aspects of our personality that cause us to hold back, fail, or never even try. It could be laziness, a lack of imagination, or deep insecurity. Spend at least five minutes probing your psyche about everything you can think of that has held you back from doing your ultimate best or being the authentic self you long to be.

Write those things here.

_____

_____

_____

_____

_____

When people criticize your behavior or traits, what do they posit as your failings? (Note: They may be entirely wrong.)

_____

_____

_____

_____

_____

_____

What aspects of your personality interfere with relationships or cause trouble at work?

_____

_____

_____

_____

_____

Is something specific holding you back from being who you are or expressing yourself freely? From pursuing your dreams?

_____

_____

_____

_____

_____

Identify the areas you need to address.

_____

_____

_____

_____

_____

_____

What Are Your Self-Limiting Beliefs?

We all have them. Far too often, we allow our limiting beliefs to forestall any forward momentum. We get stuck in our own negativity and convince ourselves that our status quo is safer. We formed them early in life and interpret everything that happens according to their tenets . . . but are they accurate?

List your top five self-limiting beliefs.

1. _____
2. _____
3. _____
4. _____
5. _____

Are these beliefs grounded in fact? If so, what are the supporting facts?

_____
_____
_____
_____
_____
_____

Did you always think that way? If not, what has changed?

_____

_____

_____

_____

_____

Is there evidence counteracting your belief?

_____

_____

_____

_____

How would you think about these beliefs if you were . . . Albert Einstein,
Oprah Winfrey, Steve Jobs, or someone you know that you consider an
astute thinker or particularly wise? Write about any insights gained by this
exercise.

_____

_____

_____

_____

Now refute your self-limiting beliefs from page 34 by writing positive statements that counteract them. What would it be like to think of the opposites to your beliefs?

1. _____

2. _____

3. _____

4. _____

5. _____

Do you think you're bright enough to branch out of your current job? What would be an aspirational job?

_____

_____

_____

_____

_____

Do you feel confident new people would respond positively to you? If not, what do you think makes this difficult?

_____

_____

_____

_____

_____

Replace Limiting Beliefs with Empowering Beliefs

Write ten statements about yourself and your capabilities that you know are true but you may have been reluctant to fully claim:

1. _____

2. _____

3. _____

4. _____

5. _____

6. _____

7. _____

8. _____

9. _____

10. _____

"You'll never know who you are unless you shed who you pretend to be."

—VIRONIKA TUGALEVA

Imagine You Are Already Who You Want to Be

Act "as if" you already possess the qualities you most desire and answer the following questions.

What would you do if you had more confidence?

_____

_____

_____

_____

_____

_____

What would you do if you knew you were a genius?

_____

_____

_____

_____

_____

_____

_____

What would you do if you knew you had exceptional talent in that area?

_____

_____

_____

_____

_____

_____

What would you do if you knew others would like and admire you for doing it?

_____

_____

_____

_____

_____

_____

What would you do if you knew you'd be wildly successful doing it?

_____

_____

_____

_____

_____

_____

What Are Your Current Personal Growth Goals?

If you don't have any personal growth goals, it's time to create some. For our purposes here, focus more on long-term, lifetime goals that you'd love to accomplish or achieve in the next five years—specifically those designed to validate, honor, and reinforce your authentic self.

What are your top five goals for the next five years?

1. _____

2. _____

3. _____

4. _____

5. _____

Do you have goals *specific* to growing as a person? What are they?

_____

_____

_____

_____

_____

_____

_____

_____

_____

What do those aspirations say about your priorities?

_____

_____

_____

_____

_____

_____

_____

_____

_____

_____

Are they in alignment with your essence, your authentic self?

_____

_____

_____

_____

_____

_____

_____

_____

_____

_____

_____

What Are Your Unmet Needs?

We all have primary physical and emotional needs, and we're all pretty much aware of what those are: food, water, shelter, sleep, intimacy, etcetera. The needs you want to focus on here are the ones that aren't currently being met. You may know exactly what they are, but if you don't, it's often what you've recently been complaining about to others. If you've been feeling bored, for example, perhaps your need for social outings or mental challenge is not being met.

Basic life needs include:

- *Safety*
- *Housing*
- *Ongoing nourishment*
- *Physical, mental, and emotional health*
- *Relationships/Intimacy*
- *Autonomy*
- *Self-determination*
- *Freedom*
- *Financial stability*
- *Respect*
- *Excitement*

Emotional needs might include:

- *Security—assurance you are free to avoid pain and gain pleasure*
- *Stimulation—mental engagement, change, new stimuli*
- *Importance—feeling unique, important, or needed*
- *Union—emotional connection with someone or something*
- *Growth—an expansion of capacity, capability, or understanding*
- *Service—contribution, helping, giving to, and supporting others*

Do you know the needs that *most* drive you? Rank them below and ponder ways you can meet them.

1. _____

2. _____

3. _____

4. _____

5. _____

6. _____

7. _____

8. _____

9. _____

10. _____

What *crucial* needs to living an authentic life are not being met?

_____

_____

_____

What can you do *right now* to address your unmet needs?

_____

_____

_____

What Are Your Wants?

What we want—from the coolest sneakers you've ever seen to world peace—tells us something about ourselves. Rather than indulge your primary wants, take time to notice what they are and what they are telling you about yourself. For instance, maybe wanting the coolest sneakers you've ever seen tells you that you value being current, fashionable, or comfortable, which may tell you that you value yourself enough to care how you present yourself to the world or that your shallow desires are masking insecurity.

Make a list of your top five current wants and then take a minute to ponder what's the driving force behind them.

1. _____

2. _____

3. _____

4. _____

5. _____

What do these desires represent?

_____

_____

_____

_____

_____

_____

_____

_____

_____

_____

What is it you *truly* want?

_____

_____

_____

_____

_____

_____

_____

_____

_____

_____

What Are Your Core Values?

Most aspects of who we are originated in our childhoods—from family, religious training, community, schooling, friendships. For example, how we adapted, what we learned about life and how to live it, what we learned about getting along with people, how to forge ahead in our lives, what living our best life looks like, and how to create goals and go after them.

For your life to be truly, authentically, yours, how you live must reflect and reinforce *your* true values. Values are anything that has deep meaning and worth to you. What you value is usually highly personal and subjective, but each culture also has values, traditions, and beliefs that influence personal values. The more you know your *own* values, the more meaning your life will have.

To get you started thinking about values, here's a list of common core values. Circle or highlight any that hold the most meaning to you.

Commitment to family	Spiritual practices	Leadership	Excellence	Expressing oneself through style
Honesty	Achievement altruism	Tradition	Courage	Faith
Self-discipline	Introspection	Exploration	Communing with nature	Fairness
Having a mission	Responsibility	Risk-taking	Mastery	Harmony
Loyalty	Nurturance	Adventure	Justice	Resilience

List any values important to you that are not on the previous chart. Or write about nuances, how the particular values from the chart manifest for you.

1. _____

2. _____

3. _____

4. _____

5. _____

Are you neglecting or negating any of the values you have circled or listed? If so, how has this affected how you feel about your life?

_____

_____

_____

_____

_____

_____

What actions can you take to incorporate the missing values?

_____

_____

_____

_____

_____

_____

Is there something you have longed to do but have yet to attempt? Why haven't you tried? What can you do to make this a priority?

_____

_____

_____

_____

_____

_____

_____

_____

_____

_____

What could you do regularly that would make you feel like an especially worthwhile person?

_____

_____

_____

_____

_____

_____

_____

_____

_____

_____

If you knew you only had a year to live, how would you spend your extremely limited, highly valuable time? (Note: This question will come up a few more times in the workbook as your answers may change.)

_____

_____

_____

_____

_____

_____

THREE BENEFITS TO HAVING STRONG CORE VALUES

1. Knowing your core values builds trust. When you know and honor your core values, they become your North Star, lighting the optimal path. The clarity you feel, knowing that you always make decisions congruent with your values, reassures you that you do your best, which builds self-confidence and reinforces trust in your ability to make solid decisions.

2. They help you endure hard times. If you practice your core values when times are good, they will serve as your backbone when times are hard. You'll be able to call on core values to know what to do, how to behave, how to weather the latest storm.

3. They improve relationships. Because you know your core values, you can also be more sensitive to others' core values. When there's conflict, you can more easily see the other person's viewpoint and settle on a compromise that honors your and their values.

Rank Your Priorities

With only about sixteen waking hours in a day, what you give precedence often reflects your true values. Take a moment to rank the following areas of your life to reflect your deepest values and core inclinations, which comes first, second, third, and so on:

	Family
	Friends
	Intimacy
	Work
	Money
	Creativity
	Spirituality

Which of the above areas receives most of your time, energy, resources, and thought? Are your priorities in alignment with your core values?

_____

_____

_____

_____

Which core values are not adequately represented in your daily life? Are you content with this ranking, or do you want to reorder your priorities?

_____

_____

_____

_____

If you want to make changes, what internal and/or external shifts are required? Who might be able to help you make desired changes?

_____

_____

_____

_____

ADDITIONAL BENEFITS TO HAVING CORE VALUES

According to *Psychological Science*, researchers repeatedly confirm that when people have a clear set of core values:

- It's easier to make big life decisions around pursuing passions, long-term career goals, and relationships.
- They are less likely to engage in destructive thought patterns, especially in difficult life situations.
- They tolerate physical pain more easily.
- They have greater self-discipline and focus when studying or working.
- Social connections are stronger.

Have You Broken from Your Parents?

To live an authentic life, it's important to determine if you're still operating from childhood beliefs, or if you have developed needs, wants, and values based on your experiences and what you have learned and chosen. To figure that out, let's review what you learned in childhood.

What did your parents *most* value?

_____

_____

_____

_____

_____

_____

Did they have a life purpose? Did they pursue it?

_____

_____

_____

_____

_____

_____

What did they model in terms of living an authentic life? Did your parents honor and nourish their souls?

_____

_____

_____

_____

_____

Did your parents see you and your unique talents accurately? Did they validate and support your genuine self? Did they encourage your individualized blossoming?

_____

_____

_____

_____

_____

Did they set up roadblocks to healthy functioning? Did they model or enable dysfunction?

_____

_____

_____

_____

_____

Review Your Adult Values

Now that you've unearthed what might have come from your parents—and perhaps remains unexamined—it's time to make sure your current values are ones you chose, from an adult perspective. Remember, if you want to live your authentic life and fulfill your life purpose, knowing who you are and what you really want to do with your life matters. Answering the following questions will help you form a clear picture of your values and whether or not you are living authentically.

How do your chosen values differ from those of your parents?

_____

_____

_____

_____

_____

_____

Have you sacrificed any values to get ahead?

_____

_____

_____

_____

_____

_____

Are you currently discounting important values?

_____

_____

_____

_____

_____

_____

_____

_____

_____

_____

We all need a reason to get up. What drives you every day?

_____

_____

_____

_____

_____

_____

_____

_____

_____

What do you have to offer that is of true value? What are your most useful strengths? What are you most suited for?

_____

_____

_____

_____

_____

Are you playing to your strengths, or do you need to go in a new direction to bolster your authentic self?

_____

_____

_____

_____

_____

Do you need to make any adjustments? Bolster any potential strengths?

_____

_____

_____

_____

_____

Do You Know Your Own Traits?

Social psychologist Kennon Sheldon believes that having *trait mindfulness*—being so aware of your feelings, desires, sensations, and emotions that you are able to observe your own and others' emotions rather than being pulled into action or reaction—helps people lead more authentic lives. Research found that people who are more mindful of their traits are more likely to pursue goals consistent with who they really are.

What are your primary traits?

_____

_____

_____

_____

_____

Are you taking advantage of them? Are you working against them?

_____

_____

_____

_____

_____

_____

Claim Your Authentic Self

This may seem premature—which is why we'll keep circling back to this essential question—but: Who are you, *really?*

Write a clear statement about who you are, what you most value in the world, and what you would do, "if" you could be your best self. Keep writing and rewriting, refining it, until what you capture sends a charge up your spine. When that happens, you're moving closer to reclaiming your authentic self and finding your life purpose.

Example:

I am a woman who feels deeply and uses her writing to express her thoughts and feelings as well as inspire others to also honor and share theirs. I care most about human connection, personal and communal growth, and mutual respect. Leaving a legacy of knowledge that helps people with similar issues live their best lives motivates me to work hard. I would love to volunteer at the local high school to teach underserved youth how to write about their lives.

> "Don't you ever let a soul in the world tell you that you can't be exactly who you are."
>
> —LADY GAGA

Now it's your turn. I am . . .

_____

_____

_____

_____

_____

_____

_____

_____

_____

_____

_____

_____

_____

_____

_____

_____

_____

By this point, you should have a clear picture of what your authentic values are, what matters most to you in terms of living your life with integrity and being faithful to your*self* and your life purpose. One of the most important steps in living an authentic life is to manage your emotions, so let's talk about how you can do that.

CHAPTER THREE

LEARN TO MANAGE YOUR EMOTIONS

To live an authentic life, it's necessary to feel what you feel, in the moment, as it happens. Unfortunately, we're often encouraged to suppress our feelings, which leads to becoming so disconnected from them that we later have trouble identifying, feeling, or expressing them.

"Be still with your quiet emotions and challenge your hard emotions."

—KIRA ASATRYAN, *STOP BEING LONELY*

Explore Your Emotional Intelligence

Emotional intelligence is reflected in how we oversee our emotions, whether we are in control of them and whether we can effectively use them to understand ourselves and others, and, equally important, whether we handle interpersonal relationships judicially and empathically. Let's answer some questions designed to shine a light on your emotional skills.

Do the people around you accurately identify and gauge your emotional states? What do they often get wrong?

_____

_____

_____

_____

_____

Do you accurately identify the emotions of those close to you? Are you aware of physical cues your beloveds use to express emotion? Examples might include a quivering lower lip when hurt and the crossing of arms when angry. Can you identify some of the cues your beloveds use?

_____

_____

_____

_____

When someone else is upset, are you able to forego reactionary responses, pause, and truly feel what the other person is feeling? Describe what you did the last time someone close to you was upset.

_____

_____

_____

_____

_____

_____

_____

_____

_____

Are you able to verbally express your caring concern? Write out a caring statement for someone who has recently expressed hurt.

_____

_____

_____

_____

_____

_____

_____

_____

_____

Do you consciously show how much you care? List ways you show those you love that you hear/see/care about their feelings.

1. _____
2. _____
3. _____
4. _____
5. _____

Imagine the last time you were with someone who was angry. Were you able to stay detached long enough to ask them calmly what was beneath the anger? What determines your ability to stay detached?

_____
_____
_____
_____
_____
_____
_____
_____
_____
_____
_____
_____
_____
_____
_____

What most often triggers your anger? What lies beneath the trigger?

_____

_____

_____

_____

_____

_____

_____

_____

_____

_____

When you are caught up in anger, how does it manifest? Do you sulk, verbally attack, punish? How have those methods worked?

_____

_____

_____

_____

_____

_____

_____

_____

_____

_____

_____

_____

What techniques have you tried for controlling your anger? Have they been effective?

_____

_____

_____

_____

_____

_____

_____

_____

_____

Write about any current frustrations. How can you phrase them in a way that will evoke understanding and compassion when you explain them to others?

_____

_____

_____

_____

_____

_____

_____

_____

_____

_____

_____

Are You Comfortable with Your Own Emotions?

You may love your emotions—perhaps not all your emotions, but most of them—or you may worry that they're often excessive or inappropriate. Take a few moments to think about your emotions and how you handle them.

Which emotions are easiest for you to feel and express?

_____

_____

_____

_____

_____

_____

Which emotions are hardest for you to feel and express?

_____

_____

_____

_____

_____

_____

_____

When was the last time you felt something strongly but didn't tell the person whose presence or actions caused the feeling? What would you say now?

_____

_____

_____

_____

_____

_____

How often is your anger productive? Think of the last time you were angry. Was it justified? Was it over the top? Do you regret expressing it?

_____

_____

_____

_____

_____

Is there something in your past that always affects how you feel and express anger? Can you put that past experience into perspective?

_____

_____

_____

_____

_____

_____

Do You Rule Your Emotions, or Do They Rule You?

Emotions happen, but how intensely they are felt and expressed is a choice you can learn to make and manage. Anger and fear can both get out of hand, dragging you far away from expressing your authentic, loving, compassionate, confident self. Here's a series of yes or no questions that will help you know if your authentic self is in charge, or if your emotions are running the show.

Do you anger quickly?	YES	NO
Is your anger usually based on what's happening in the present, or is it often compounded by past experiences?	YES	NO
Can you tame heated emotions in the moment?	YES	NO
Once bitten, do you remain angry, hurt, insulted, or spiteful?	YES	NO
Are you often so frustrated it affects your productivity?	YES	NO
Does fear prevent you from doing things you'd love to do?	YES	NO
Do you fall into emotional pits that drag on and on?	YES	NO
Have emotional outbursts damaged crucial relationships?	YES	NO

If you've answered yes to many of the above questions, emotional management skills are in order.

Strive for Emotional Mastery

Emotional mastery means accepting, embracing, experiencing, and managing your emotions—be they soft or challenging. Emotions keep your conscious mind in touch with your deepest feelings, values, and purpose. Authentic people have the ability to remain calm and levelheaded no matter how difficult the situation, which allows them to make better decisions. Here are six ways to master your emotions:

1. Notice how the emotion feels in your body. *Warmth in the heart region. Tenseness in your jaw. Thumping in your head. A flood of warmth throughout your body. Lightness, or a floaty feeling.*

2. Nonjudgmentally, consciously, feel the feeling. *The more you allow feelings to run their course, the more you'll open yourself to feeling all your feelings as they happen.*

3. Identify and name it. *Is it sadness, anger, affection, joy, terror? You can start with major emotions, but work towards narrowing it down to something specific, and, when possible, specific to what caused the emotion. This widens your range of feelings.*

4. Express it in words. *The more you learn to express how you are feeling in words, even if you're alone, the more it will help you learn to tell others how you are feeling, which bolsters intimacy.*

5. Gauge its power. *While it's desirable to feel what you're feeling, when you feel it, it's not always an accurate reading of what you feel. Feelings directed towards another can irreparably harm relationships and often it's wise to let overheated emotions cool before venting.*

6. Choose how to respond. *Learning to calm your emotions, avoid overreaction, and directly address what caused them are skills we'll discuss throughout this chapter.*

Learn to Tame Difficult Emotions

Often, the intensity of difficult feelings has little to do with what's happening in that moment. Instead, the escalation of feelings is affected by deep-seated issues. This means, if your emotions run so high that you feel out of control, you are likely responding to something that happened long ago—and perhaps keeps happening. In this situation, learning to tame your emotions helps you regain control.

To tame your emotions, learn to separate your*self* from the emotion. You are not the anger you feel. The emotion is a *feeling* coursing through you, which may run its course if you allow yourself to simply feel it sans judgment or suppression. Feeling it does not mean expressing it outwardly. It simply means feeling how the emotion manifests within your body, identifying the emotion with the realization that emotions can manifest in odd ways—anger can actually be grief, for example—and then purposefully releasing the emotion.

Emotions happen, often outside of your ability to control them. What you can control, however, is how intense you allow the emotion to become and how you modulate its expression. For example, you can control intensity by removing yourself from the situation for a few minutes, literally moving out of the line of fire until you've calmed yourself; you can find a quiet place to experience the feeling, identify the feeling, and purposefully calm yourself. Once calm, you'll be able to modulate your emotions, keeping them appropriate to the current situation. So let's discuss specific ways to tame your emotions.

Try Breathing

When emotions feel out of control, or a minor situation is triggering an overblown response, pausing to calm yourself will improve emotional mastery. If at all possible, find a space where you can quiet your raging emotions. Then spend at least five minutes focused solely on slowly drawing breaths in, from deep in your abdomen, to the count of ten; holding them for another ten; then steadily releasing them counting down from ten.

Once you feel calmer, assess how much of the emotion you're feeling belongs to the current situation and how much belongs to another time, another frustration, something unrelated to what's happening now.

Then, turn your thoughts inward. What is this feeling *really* about? Is your reaction fair? Are you being fair to the other person? To yourself? If not, wait until you are able to quiet inflated emotions, then calmly address the underlying cause with the appropriate person.

"Managing your emotions doesn't mean you don't express yourself; it means you stop short of hurting others and sabotaging yourself."

—SUE FITZMAURICE

Try Meditation

Meditation is a helpful method for understanding and modulating your emotions. While it's hard to do in the heat of an argument or when you're upset for other reasons, as a daily practice learning to meditate can help you master your emotions. All that meditation requires is:

- *A quiet place where you can sit in peace, either cross-legged on the floor or in a chair with your feet grounded on the floor.*
- *Breathing slowly in and out until you feel calm, focusing all thoughts on your breath until your mind quiets.*
- *Focusing your attention for five to ten minutes solely on what's happening in your body and mind.*
- *Recognizing, acknowledging, then releasing thoughts and feelings as they arise. Try seeing your thoughts and feelings as butterflies that lightly land then flit away.*

If you need guidance, you can find free guided meditations online. Over time, when meditating, you will likely encounter your problematic emotions. Simply note which ones occur most often, which ones have the most "heat," then release them. Journal later about the emotions and what might be their root cause.

Try a meditation focused on your emotions now. Simply sit quietly, breathing slowly in and out for a few minutes, and allow any emotions to arise. After you complete five to ten minutes of focusing solely on your feelings—identifying, acknowledging, then releasing them—turn the page and answer the questions.

"Meditation trains our inner world. It is the art of creating a space between your breath and thoughts, a space that allows you to choose your own response. That allows us to overcome stimuli and reactions, so we can choose who we want to be, moment to moment."

—NATASHA POTTER

Which emotions arose, and which ones demanded the most attention?

_____

_____

_____

_____

_____

_____

_____

_____

_____

How did your body feel when they arose?

_____

_____

_____

_____

_____

_____

_____

_____

_____

_____

_____

_____

How did your mind respond?

_____

_____

_____

_____

_____

_____

_____

_____

_____

_____

_____

Did you immediately judge your emotions as unacceptable? Was that response helpful? Is there a better way to respond?

_____

_____

_____

_____

_____

_____

_____

_____

_____

_____

_____

Try Mindfulness

Quite simply, mindfulness is using your senses to focus your attention on what is happening, or what you are doing in the moment. If you were mindfully preparing carrots for dinner, for example, you would notice how they feel in your hands, their bright orange color, how they smell, how cold the water feels as you wash them, how lightly your sharp knife slices through them, the sound they make as you drop them into a pan, and how eagerly you await the chance to eat them. While paying attention, all thoughts would be on the specific actions you are taking and an appreciation of sensations—including feelings!—that arise.

Practicing mindfulness helps you keep your brain focused and grounded, which clears your mind, allowing you to be more open and thereby more authentic. You can incorporate small moments of mindfulness into your daily life by tuning in to your senses while performing routine tasks or by doing a mindfulness meditation after a particularly stressful situation. You could also try a mindful walking exercise or a guided meditation— you can find a multitude of free and paid ones online.

Pause now to focus solely on your breath until feelings arise. Take note of them, then actively release them.

Which feelings popped up?

_____

_____

_____

_____

_____

_____

How intensely did you feel them?

_____

_____

_____

_____

_____

MINDFULNESS BOOSTS AUTHENTICITY

An Australian study of more than 800 people
revealed that practicing mindfulness may
be associated with living more authentically.
Researchers found that subjects who were identified
as being more mindful lived in alignment with their
values and thus experienced greater well being.

How did your body feel while experiencing them?

_____

_____

_____

_____

_____

_____

_____

_____

_____

_____

_____

PLAY THREE QUESTIONS

When emotions catch you by surprise and threaten to overwhelm you, take a few slow, deep breaths and ask yourself these three simple questions:

1. What am I feeling?
2. Why am I feeling this way?
3. What will it take to help me feel at peace with this situation?

These questions will help you calm your emotions, assess their validity, and then address the underlying issue in a measured, healthy manner.

TAKE MINDFUL MOMENTS

When you feel stressed, try a quick check-in. Find a quiet spot where you can close your eyes and focus on your breath. Are you breathing deeply or are your breaths shallow? Are you holding tension in your face, neck, shoulders, or belly? Spend ten to fifteen seconds focused on breathing deeply, releasing any tension, and then slowly refocus on what's happening in the present moment.

How did it feel to release them?

_____

_____

_____

_____

_____

_____

_____

_____

_____

_____

_____

_____

_____

The more you practice mindfulness in relation to your emotions, the more skillful you will become at moderating and expressing them.

What's Behind Your Emotions?

To contain your emotions, pause to examine the real, underlying issue. Often, old resentments create a feeling of being trampled upon that escalates emotion. Once you identify the real issue behind your emotion—and whether it's appropriate to what's happening in the moment—you can limit distortion and choose to respond appropriately. Managing emotions means examining what's coming solely from your own heart, accepting responsibility for your feelings, then addressing the issue in a nonaccusatory manner.

Think of the last time you were furious with a loved one. What emotions occurred? How did they feel in your body?

_____

_____

_____

_____

How did you express your anger? What did you say? How did you say it?

_____

_____

_____

_____

Did your statements/actions capture what you truly felt?

_____

_____

_____

_____

_____

_____

_____

Were old resentments or other issues clouding the issue, amplifying it out of proportion? Did old anger override what just happened in the present moment? Were you consciously aware of the overreaction in the moment?

_____

_____

_____

_____

_____

_____

_____

Learning to manage your emotions requires you to identify them, own them, keep them relevant to the current situation, and express them in a calm, clear, _nonaccusatory_ manner.

Avoid the Blame Game

Often when we are angry or upset, we blame the other person. Their behavior may have triggered a response, but a fully realized, authentic response would involve taking responsibility for your emotions. Instead of lashing out with accusatory statements focused on the other person's behavior, it's important to make I statements that express *how* you feel not *why* you feel.

Ideally, rather than attack the other person, you make a definitive emotional assessment, then clearly identify what you were *really* angry about and why. An example would be: My sister rarely makes time for me, and when she does, she's distracted or so stressed she snaps at me, which makes me angry. The last time this happened, I yelled: "You never make time for me!" and stormed off.

While the true, definitive emotional statement would be: When my sister doesn't make time for me, I feel I'm not a special person in her life. When she doesn't stop fidgeting or looking at her phone, I feel I'm not important enough for her to pay attention, which leaves me feeling abandoned and lonely. I often felt this way when our parents were too busy to notice my distress.

Take three examples from your life and write the true emotional statements behind your anger, frustration, or hurt feelings.

1. _____

2. _____

3. _____

Write what you would say to the other person now. Take responsibility for your feelings.

1. _____

2. _____

3. _____

Have You Mastered Your Emotions?

Here's a short yes or no quiz to see if you've achieved emotional mastery.

Are you in alignment with your emotions?	YES	NO
Are your emotions integrated, and appropriate for what's happening in your life?	YES	NO
When deep-seated emotions arise, can you manage them?	YES	NO
Do you have ongoing, healthy, reciprocal relationships?	YES	NO
Do you freely express your genuine emotions?	YES	NO
Do you speak up when the inciting incident happens, or wait until later?	YES	NO

If you answered yes to all of the above, you're well on your way to mastery. If you had a few no answers, you've got more work to do—and that's okay. It's time to ponder what is making you feel so vulnerable.

Write about any realizations you had after taking the previous quiz about mastering your emotions. What areas do you still need to address?

_____

_____

_____

_____

_____

_____

_____

_____

_____

_____

_____

_____

_____

_____

_____

_____

_____

_____

_____

_____

_____

_____

_____

_____

What Are Your Vulnerabilities?

All of us have vulnerable aspects of our personalities—clinically known as neuroses, more accurately described as quirky behavior based on unmet needs. Often these may be seen as odd things we say or do that cause some disruption in relationships. Maybe you obsess about cleanliness to the point you make others nervous about being in your home? Maybe you're forgetful and always late? Maybe you get so focused on what you're doing you don't notice someone else is standing right next to you crying?

The vulnerability behind the behavior likely stems from worrying that you're not good enough or lovable enough or smart enough. Often these vulnerabilities are the things about us we try to hide from new acquaintances as long as we can. Here's the space to write about them with brutal honesty.

What are the vulnerable aspects of your personality, the ones that cause the most problems?

1.

2.

3.

4.

5.

How do the vulnerable aspects of your personality manifest?

1. _____

2. _____

3. _____

4. _____

5. _____

Can you identify the unmet needs that first created these vulnerabilities?

1. _____

2. _____

3. _____

4. _____

5. _____

> "Honesty and transparency make you vulnerable. Be honest and transparent anyway."
>
> —MOTHER THERESA

Are these unmet needs still happening? Is the way you behave when feeling frustrated warranted or effective? What new steps could you take to address your vulnerabilities?

1. _____

2. _____

3. _____

4. _____

5. _____

There are often *positive* aspects to vulnerabilities. Do yours make you more sensitive? Capable of incredible focus? Efficient and capable? Reliable?

FLIP IT

A vulnerability can hide a strength. For example, if you're someone who overthinks or obsesses about every detail, maybe it's a superpower because, in actuality, you're someone who sees all, anticipates all, addresses all. If you're bossy and demanding, in actuality you're a leader capable of amazing focus and decisiveness. Take one of your vulnerabilities and try flipping it.

Are You Confronting *Self*-Limiting Fears?

Fear-based thinking often locks a person in place, preventing the kind of growth and expansion that living an authentic life requires. Assessing whether fears, those holding you back from full expression of your*self*, are genuine becomes a useful skill.

Genuine fear is a reaction to a genuine threat. It has a physical component that motivates action—for example, racing heart, adrenaline rush, impulse to flee.

False fear is not based on a current threat, but nevertheless creates anxiety or worry and may paralyze you. It is often learned in childhood thanks to an overbearing or punishing authority figure, such as a parent or teacher, who wouldn't tolerate certain emotions, like anger.

If you feel fearful, it's important to gather information and determine whether the situation is genuinely fear-inducing or if you are experiencing a false fear.

What sparks fear in your life?

Have you noticed a pattern of fearfulness? Can you trace it back to your childhood? What occurrences or beliefs might be at its root?

_____

_____

_____

_____

_____

_____

What are you currently afraid of doing? What makes this a fearful possibility?

_____

_____

_____

_____

_____

If it's fake fear, what steps can you take to address the fear head-on?

_____

_____

_____

_____

_____

Do you need any prior preparation before moving forward? How can you acquire whatever it is you need?

_____

_____

_____

_____

If you were feeling particularly courageous, what would you do right now?

_____

_____

_____

_____

BEFRIEND YOUR FEAR OF FAILURE

While Buddha spent his long night under the Bodhi tree meditating, the Shadow God Mara—representing greed, hatred, delusion—tried everything to make him fail in his quest, sending violent storms, temptresses, demons, and massive armies. Buddha ignored it all, and, even after he became a fully realized being, he would often sense Mara watching from the perimeter. Instead of responding with anger, fear, or reactivity, he would calmly say, "I see you, Mara, let's have tea."

If Mara is your burgeoning fear of failure, do you succumb to his taunts? Or do you calmly acknowledge his presence and invite him to tea? Rather than recoil in fear or defensiveness, try responding with clarity, graciousness, and ease.

If you had $10 million in cash, perfect health, and no restrictions—such as a job, spouse, children to consider—what would you *do* with your most precious time?

_____

_____

_____

_____

_____

_____

_____

_____

Here it is again: If you only had one year to live, what would you desperately want to do? Think of things that would finally reflect and fulfill your innermost self.

_____

_____

_____

_____

_____

_____

_____

_____

THINK ABUNDANCE!

When you focus on positives in your life and feel genuine gratitude for your blessings, it helps you develop an abundance mindset in which you trust that your needs will be met and see beauty and goodness all around you. This confidence that your future needs will be met helps you stay focused on what's happening in the present moment. Your life becomes an exciting journey, one that attracts more positivity and joy. Here's how you know you have an abundance mindset:

- You celebrate others' successes. No one else's success detracts from your own because you know your time will come.
- You're generous in all aspects of your life, often volunteering your time, energy, or skills. You trust everything you need will be available when you need it.
- You live in the present moment. You put the past behind you and let the future unfold.

Now, ponder this: What could you do that would induce deep inner joy? Think about it and see if you can answer the following questions:

- *Where would you go?*
- *How would you live?*
- *What would you do to make yourself happy?*
- *What would make you feel like the most worthwhile person on the planet?*
- *What do you truly think would bring you the greatest fulfillment?*

Now that you've mastered your emotions and addressed any fear that may be holding you back from living your authentic life, let's talk about compassion.

CHAPTER FOUR

DEVELOP COMPASSION

The pace and complexity of our modern world has not only blunted our ability to enjoy a rich emotional life, but its demands make the kind of genuine connection that living authentically desires difficult to achieve. We have to consciously extend ourselves and draw others out to create intimacy. Compassion is an essential tool for being open and honest in reciprocal relationships, and thereby living authentically.

"You yourself, as much as anybody in the entire universe, deserve your love and affection."

—SHARON SALZBERG

The five central aspects of compassion are:

1. *Generosity*
2. *Hospitality*
3. *Objectivity*
4. *Sensitivity*
5. *Tolerance across social networks and relationships*

Each is essential to living an authentic life. Living authentically means offering compassion to your*self* as well as to others.

THREE WAYS TO OFFER YOUR*SELF* COMPASSION

Rather than berate yourself for perceived mistakes, use these three simple steps to offer yourself compassion:

1. Take responsibility for the minor screwup.
2. Forgive yourself for being human.
3. Make amends, right the wrong, and create a system for doing better.

Being compassionate towards your own behavior allows your authentic self to blossom and grow.

Do You Offer Yourself Compassion?

We all make mistakes. Fortunately, most of our mistakes are minor and often easily reparable. If you forgot someone's birthday, didn't return a favor, or said something hurtful, a genuine apology often rectifies your atypical behavior. While it's important to hold yourself accountable—and rectify the situation—it's not productive to assume you're a bad person who's constantly screwing up.

Keeping who you are separate from the minor mistakes you've made validates your simple humanity and allows you to learn how to do better. Using minor screwups to berate yourself and make yourself feel guilty or ashamed is inappropriate and nonproductive. Let's see if you're offering your*self* the kind of compassion that fosters growth.

What do you tend to berate yourself for doing?

_____

_____

_____

_____

_____

_____

_____

_____

Do you have a negative soundtrack that secretly plays in your mind—one that limits your development? How does this hold you back?

_____

_____

_____

_____

_____

_____

_____

How could you offer yourself compassion for what you may have perceived as failings?

_____

_____

_____

_____

_____

_____

_____

_____

_____

_____

One vital way to take care of your*self* is to forgive yourself for transgressions. Focus on perceived errors in judgment or actions that have prevented you from being your authentic self and answer the following questions.

What have you done lately that seemed like an egregious mistake? List any that have held you back from living an authentic life.

_____

_____

_____

_____

_____

_____

_____

_____

_____

_____

_____

_____

> "Relationships require complete integrity. The first time you lie or are untrue to your partner, you condemn yourself and your partner to a second-class relationship. First-class relationships are possible only in an atmosphere of total trust."
>
> —WU WEI, *I CHING LIFE: BECOMING YOUR AUTHENTIC SELF*

Is this something you often do? Does it make you feel like a failure? Do you berate or punish yourself? If so, how?

_____

_____

_____

_____

_____

_____

_____

_____

_____

_____

Write a few sentences expressing forgiveness to yourself. Can you now release any harsh judgments towards yourself?

_____

_____

_____

_____

_____

_____

_____

_____

_____

_____

_____

Are You Connecting with Others?

Knowing how to extend yourself and express yourself—without offending or wounding others—is something we all need to learn, particularly if we want to be our authentic selves. A healthy, highly functioning, fully realized adult also wants authentic relationships in which all parties are fully being and expressing who they are. Let's see how you're doing with relationships.

Do you socialize regularly? How often?

_____

_____

_____

_____

_____

_____

_____

_____

_____

_____

_____

_____

_____

_____

AUTHENTICITY ATTRACTS OTHERS

Authentic people attract others as they tend to:

- Put themselves in other people's shoes and see the world from their perspective.
- Easily find common ground with others regardless of how different they may be.
- Make others comfortable sharing their vulnerable side.
- Respect everyone, even when they disagree.
- Know that everyone has something valuable to offer and that we can learn from each other.
- See the good in others, even when they cannot see it in themselves.
- Be drawn to helping others because they understand what it feels like to need help.

Thus, authentic people also make great leaders and are highly sought after in business, politics, and spiritual realms.

Do you have a group of intimate friends? List them. What makes each a genuine connection?

1. _____

2. _____

3. _____

4. _____

5. _____

Do you fully trust your friends? Do you share your deepest emotions with them? Do you hide anything? Why? What have you been hiding? Why?

_____

_____

_____

_____

_____

_____

_____

_____

_____

_____

_____

MODEL AUTHENTICITY

When all parties feel safe enough to share genuine feelings, a reciprocal relationship becomes authentic. If you believe that someone really cares about you—that it's neither transactional nor driven by expectation but truly and freely offered from the heart—it feels authentic, trustworthy, dependable, comforting, and loving. The more you model open and honest sharing, the stronger your relationship will become.

Do you have a confidante, someone you truly trust with your darkest secrets and most stultifying fears? What have you told this person about your secret yearnings? Your life purpose?

_____

_____

_____

_____

_____

_____

_____

_____

_____

_____

_____

_____

_____

ENCOURAGE RECIPROCAL INTIMACY

If someone never talks about their past, gently invite them to do so. Try saying: "I notice that you rarely talk about your childhood. Is there a reason?" Or try saying: "I've shared some of my major setbacks, but you've never told me about yours. Would you care to share?"

Can You Listen with Detachment?

To be consciously compassionate, when someone is telling you an emotional story, it's best to remain detached enough to remain objective. This helps you see and address what's most important to the person sharing. One way you could achieve this is by imagining what the person describes as a movie or novel, about which you'd be thinking:

- *What was the setting?*
- *What was the emotional temperature?*
- *Who were the characters?*
- *What were the characters upset about and why?*
- *What were each character's underlying motivations?*
- *Was anyone being unreasonable in this situation?*
- *Were the wounded party's feelings justified?*
- *Can I see this story solely through the storyteller's point of view?*

Now, let's give it a try. Think back to the last argument someone recounted to you and analyze it using the guidelines above.

What was the setting? What was the emotional temperature? Who were the characters?

_____

_____

_____

_____

_____

What were the characters upset about and why? What were each character's underlying motivations?

_____

_____

_____

_____

_____

Was anyone being unreasonable in this situation? Were the wounded party's feelings justified?

_____

_____

_____

_____

_____

Could you see what happened solely through the sharer's eyes? What would you say to the person sharing?

_____

_____

_____

_____

_____

Now, think back to the last time you were upset with someone and analyze that situation in an objective manner.

What was the setting? What was the emotional temperature? Who were the characters?

_____

_____

_____

_____

_____

What were the characters upset about and why? What were each character's underlying motivations?

_____

_____

_____

_____

Was anyone being unreasonable in this situation? Were the wounded party's feelings justified?

_____

_____

_____

_____

Were you able to see the situation from the other person's point of view? What would you say to them now?

_____

_____

_____

_____

REPETITION REVEALS

When someone tells you the same painful story over and over, they likely have unresolved issues related to the story itself. Always listen but, at some point, it's okay to gently ask:

- What is this story really about?
- What does this story mean to you?
- How does telling this story benefit you?
- What needs to happen to lessen its negative impact?

Note: This can also apply to you and the stories you tell.

Are You Truly Listening?

To live authentically, you need to hear—and honor—what others are saying. However, we've all been in conversations when we know the other person isn't really listening. We all know how not being heard hurts, particularly when you are attempting to tell someone you love something important, something that makes you feel vulnerable. Active listening is essential to having authentic relationships.

Here's how to truly listen and help the other person feel seen and heard:

1. *Focus on the person's eyes while listening closely to their words. Body language often sheds light on what the other person is feeling, but looking directly into their eyes encourages intimacy.*

2. *Restate what the person just told you as accurately as you can. This both lets the person know you heard them and, if their meaning wasn't clear, gives them an opportunity to rephrase it.*

3. *Reframe their statement. If it's angry, try to soften it. If it's too narrow, expand it. Do this gently to help the speaker decide if they are reflecting true thoughts or caught up in an emotional reaction.*

4. *Reflect what they are telling you through actions. If they have been wringing their hands or biting their lip while talking, telling them what you see may offer valuable feedback on the speaker's true emotions.*

5. *Summarize what you heard, noting any overarching theme. This helps a close friend or relative have a broader perspective.*

6. *Validate their experience by expressing that you understand and can relate to what they have been talking about. This reassures the person that they are making sense and they are safe in sharing with you.*

Ideally, after you have remained quiet while listening closely to someone talk about something that's painful or traumatic for them, you would ask these essential questions:

- *How does that make you feel?*
- *What needs to happen to make it feel better?*
- *What can you do to effect change?*
- *How can I support you?*

These questions reflect genuine concern and the kind of support that fosters authenticity.

Further, when someone comes to you with a situation in which they feel that you have wronged them, rather than barraging them with questions to find out what and why, try inviting them to share. Avoid making assumptions, avoid any leading questions, and listen *carefully* to the emotions being expressed.

ALWAYS ASK BEFORE SHARING

It's not your responsibility to resolve someone else's situation. Remaining attentive yet detached allows you to objectively view the situation. Once the storyteller's emotions have subsided, you may have objective observations to offer, but *ask* if the storyteller is interested in hearing them first.

Do You *Feel* Empathy?

Empathy is the ability to genuinely *feel* what another person is feeling, to see and experience their situation purely from their perspective rather than your own. It differs from sympathy, in which one is moved by the thoughts and feelings of another but maintains an emotional distance. When you verbally respond to how a person is feeling with obvious care and concern—which comes from feeling empathy—the person feels seen, heard, and loved.

Generally, emotions reflect an intensity:

Soft emotions tend to make a person more accessible. These often include happiness, sadness, joy, regret, remorse, admiration, trust, grief, and pain. If you're being empathic with soft emotions, it's usually fine to just "be with" the person. To draw even closer and show the person you care, perhaps try touching their arm, offering a hug, making them a cup of tea, or putting a strong hand on their shoulder.

Hard emotions tend to erect walls between people. They include anger, fear, distrust, jealousy, contempt, and worry. If you're attempting to be empathic with someone caught in hard emotions, how you respond to their behavior may create distance.

"True closeness can only be achieved through authenticity, openness, and empathy."

—STEFANIE STAHL, *THE CHILD IN YOU: THE BREAKTHROUGH METHOD FOR BRINGING OUT YOUR AUTHENTIC SELF*

When hard emotions are expressed, it's important to remain neutral and meet the intensity of the person's emotions with a direct challenge to the genuineness of the emotion. This is not done to negate the emotion but solely to challenge the *true* source of the emotion. In essence, you gently ask them what is *really* beneath the anger, frustration, jealousy they're feeling—for example, "I see you are angry, but I'm wondering what is really behind this feeling." What you hope is that the person will be able to look inward and share from a place of authenticity. If that happens, both parties will feel closer.

If you don't know how to feel and express empathy, follow these steps:

1. *Use verbal and nonverbal cues to assess and identify the other person's emotion.*
2. *Tamp down your own reactionary responses and pause to physically feel their emotion in your body.*
3. *Genuinely respond in a concerned way, both verbally and by doing something to show you care.*

Ideally, empathy becomes a relational muscle you can develop to deepen authentic relationships.

DEPOSIT LOVE REGULARLY

If you compare relationships to a bank account in which both parties make deposits, is yours overdrawn? Sustainable relationships blossom when acts of love are consistently deposited into "an account" one can draw upon when needed. It's also important to hold yourself responsible. Are you making love deposits to your private account?

Do You Foster Authentic Intimacy?

When you live an authentic life, you tend to attract like-minded people. But to deepen and maintain relationships, you need to offer sustained, escalating, reciprocal, personal self-disclosure. Sharing your opinions and true thoughts on important subjects reinforces your authenticity and bolsters genuine intimacy.

Intimacy occurs when your *innermost* self feels validated, valued, and cared for by someone else. Authentic intimacy means being able to be fully yourself and be seen and understood by others. Ideally, friends feel their authentic self is seen, understood, and valued by each other. When people close to us don't "get" us, it undermines intimacy.

If you present a social self that you think is more appealing, you run the risk of limiting intimacy. We all like to be admired, but, if we also don't feel "truly seen," it may feel incongruous with who we think we are. When others see us as more confident and successful than we are, for example, it can create distance, when what we truly want is to feel understood by and close to others.

Intimacy involves sharing to be known, without attachment to the outcome, and listening with curiosity to find out who the other person is, without defensiveness. Reciprocation is a key element to creating intimacy.

Are you comfortable sharing hurtful events from your past with friends? Why or why not?

_____

_____

_____

_____

_____

Are there secrets you never share, even with friends you trust? What are they? Why do they feel like something you should hide?

_____

_____

_____

_____

_____

TAKE TURNS

Relationships require trust and sharing. To foster trust and encourage greater intimacy, always make space for the other person to share. Try thinking of social situations like tennis matches. Sometimes the ball is in your court, and other times you purposefully serve it to your companion. When it's time to share, be willing to share your inner *self* and make it feel safe for them to reciprocate.

Do You Have Authentic Friendships?

According to research published in *Personality and Social Psychology Bulletin*, there's a phenomenon called *acceptance prophecy*. When you *assume* that others like you, you become warmer, friendlier, and more open. This makes others like you, creating a self-fulfilling prophecy that you'd be eagerly welcomed and accepted.

That said, if you're presenting a social self, or false front, you won't know if they'll also like your authentic self. The good news is that being authentic attracts others to you, particularly those with similar values. Plus, once you realize your true potential, you'll find you have the respect of others as well as yourself.

So, how are your friendships? Do you have intimate, reciprocal relationships in which all parties are authentically themselves? One way to know is to ask yourself some essential questions.

Whom do you most trust when it comes to sharing your authentic self?

_____

_____

_____

_____

_____

_____

Who shares their authentic, *innermost* self with you?

_____

_____

_____

_____

_____

_____

Which of your friendships are genuinely reciprocal?

_____

_____

_____

_____

_____

_____

Whom do you learn from?

_____

_____

_____

_____

_____

_____

Who challenges you?

_____

_____

_____

_____

_____

Whom do you feel most comfortable confiding your darkest secrets or scariest fears to?

_____

_____

_____

_____

_____

_____

With whom do you find joy?

_____

_____

_____

_____

_____

_____

Authentic friends should reflect back something that is admirable or aspirational, something you want to achieve. What do you most admire about your closest friends?

_____

_____

_____

_____

_____

_____

_____

_____

_____

_____

_____

_____

_____

> "You have to try to help people understand and accept you, which conversely means you have to understand and accept yourself enough that you believe you can make somebody else's life brighter just by being in it."
>
> —DONALD MILLER

Are Your Friendships Solid?

It's difficult to foster intimacy between friends if you don't have a secure foundation, the level of trust that makes it easy for you to share your innermost thoughts and concerns. Dr. Amir Levine, author of *Attached: The New Science of Adult Attachment and How It Can Help You Find and Keep Love*, identified five foundational elements of secure relationships:

1. Consistency: *Do these friends drift in and out of my life on a whim?*
2. Availability: *How available are they to spend time together?*
3. Reliability: *Can I count on them if I need something?*
4. Responsiveness: *Do they reply to my emails and texts? Do I hear from them on a consistent basis?*
5. Predictability: *Can I count on them to act in a certain way?*

Let's see if your friendships are on solid ground. Using the CARRP standard above, answer the following questions:

Who are your five closest friends?

1. _____

2. _____

3. _____

4. _____

5. _____

Do you feel this level of security in each of those relationships? If not, why? Are you holding up your end? What can you do to solidify your most important friendships?

_____

_____

_____

_____

_____

_____

_____

_____

_____

_____

_____

_____

_____

_____

_____

"When you're authentic, you end up following your heart, and you put yourself in places and situations and in conversations that you love and that you enjoy. You meet people that you like talking to. You go places you've dreamt about. And you end up following your heart and feeling very fulfilled."

—NEIL PASRICHA

What Do You Do to Maintain Friendships?

When you are living authentically, you often attract friends easily, but relationships only deepen and grow if you nurture them. Here's how to maintain and deepen friendships:

- See each other consistently. *Make time for your friends each week.*
- Be fully present. *When you're with them, give them your full attention.*
- Be genuine. *True intimacy only comes when you share your authentic self.*
- Be there when they need you. *Always reach out when you know they are facing challenges.*
- Celebrate special occasions. *Milestones matter and celebrating them together reinforces bonds.*
- Do fun things together. *People frequently grow closer when they are relaxed and enjoying being with each other. Plus, happy memories are bonding memories.*
- Do expansive things together. *Encouraging each other to grow is one of the most important aspects of loving someone.*
- Be generous. *Thoughtful gifts show that they matter, as do smaller gestures. Texting them a quotation they'll love or something to make them laugh fosters connection.*

Are you doing what's needed to maintain your most important friendships? List five specific things you can do to let your most important friends know how much you value them.

1. _____

2. _____

3. _____

4. _____

5. _____

TAKE FIVE!

Offering a friend five minutes of your undivided attention is often enough to nurture the relationship. When face to face, put everything down, focus on their eyes, listen closely, and respond with love. You can also simply take five minutes to call a dear friend, just to check in and let them know you're thinking about them.

Are You Fully Present for Friends in Need?

Elizabeth Scott, author of *8 Keys to Stress Management*, suggested five basic steps when listening to a friend in need:

1. Listen closely. *Maintain eye contact with your friend, stay present, and show them you're interested in what they have to say.*

2. Repeat key details. *When we summarize and repeat key details back to someone, they feel heard. "It looks like things are becoming hostile" and "You sound like you're feeling hurt" are two examples of what to say when your friend is sharing a difficult story or conflict.*

3. Focus on feelings. *When you don't know what to say, rather than repeatedly discussing the details of the situation ask, "What are you feeling about what happened?*

4. Keep the focus on them. *It's okay to say you can relate or to share a few details about your own experience, but don't shift the focus of the conversation to your situation and feelings. Keep the focus on your friend's situation.*

5. Brainstorm. *Rather than offering advice, gently generate a brainstorming session to find solutions. Try asking: What do you want to do about this? How does that make you feel? Do you see any other options?*

Do you have the previous skills? If not, which ones do you need to strengthen?

_____

_____

_____

_____

_____

_____

_____

_____

_____

_____

CULTIVATE JOY

We can increase our joy by sharing others' joy. Try asking: "What was the bright spot of your day?" or "What's the best thing that happened to you this week?" Asking about other people's wins turns you into a joy spectator, giving you a chance to witness them at their best.

Now that we've talked about how to foster authentic relationships, it's time to evaluate your ability to honor your authentic self by always speaking your truth.

CHAPTER FIVE

LIVE WITH INTEGRITY AND TAKE RESPONSIBILITY

When you live with integrity, you choose to stay in alignment with your values and instinctively do what is right versus what is convenient. You value and maintain focus on your bigger dreams, desires, and objectives. It also means living in congruence with a higher self—a philosophical viewpoint or personal code. Those with integrity have a strong personal code that they honor. If you live with integrity, you love and support your authentic self, which helps your life feel fluid and honorable.

"Believing things that aren't true for us at the deepest level is the commonest way in which we lose our integrity. Then suffering arises...to help us locate our internal divisions, reclaim our reality, and heal these inner rifts."

—MARTHA BECK, *THE WAY OF INTEGRITY*

Integrity Checklist

If you are living a life of integrity, in confluence with your authentic self, you:

- [x] Know who you are and what matters most to you.
- [x] Take deliberate action.
- [x] Avoid reactivity. You pause to consider possible outcomes, then choose to do what fits your moral code or your long-term life goals.
- [x] Trust yourself—and your personal code.
- [x] Choose what's right for you, whether or not your family or friends agree.
- [x] Keep your feet on solid ground.
- [x] Think independently and decide what feels right.
- [x] Hold strong to your own beliefs. You've given thought to what you think and have a personal philosophy that guides your behavior.
- [x] Strive to be the best you can be.
- [x] Take full responsibility when you screw up.
- [x] Feel in charge of your life, and thus don't blame others if things go awry.
- [x] See setbacks as opportunities to learn.
- [x] Don't report to anyone and feel free to live your life.

How are you doing on the above checklist? Note some areas you need to work on and brainstorm ways to address them.

_____

_____

_____

_____

Have You Established Boundaries?

Consciously or unconsciously, we create boundaries—real or imagined lines—that tell us what we will and will not tolerate in our own or others' behavior. Boundaries also establish what we need to feel loved as well as fully alive, fulfilled, and happy. You may not have consciously thought about your boundaries, but to live a life of integrity, it's important to know what they are—and perhaps to adjust them.

What are your primary boundaries—"thou shalts"—in love, work, and family?

_____

_____

_____

_____

_____

> "Living from a place of authenticity is difficult because those living in distortion see you as a threat to their delusion and some are so attached to that delusion that they will behave in erratic ways to defend their ego's projection of wounding."
>
> —SUZANNE WAGNER

What are your primary boundaries—"thou shalt nots"—in love, work, and family?

_____

_____

_____

_____

_____

_____

_____

_____

_____

_____

Are your boundaries in sync with your most important and adult values?

_____

_____

_____

_____

_____

_____

_____

_____

_____

_____

Where do you absolutely draw the boundary line, and is it time to rethink any boundary lines?

_____

_____

_____

_____

_____

_____

_____

What's your philosophical ideal or personal code—guideline for optimal behavior—at work, at home, with extended family, with friends? To create personal codes, perhaps go back to chapter 2 and review your core values. A personal code for work might be: I treat myself and others with mutual respect on all matters, and I expect others to offer me reciprocal trust and respect.

_____

_____

_____

_____

_____

_____

_____

Do You Maintain Your Boundaries?

Boundaries are healthy tools used to maintain your sense of who you are by setting parameters for what's acceptable and what's not acceptable. They help you separate and own what's yours and return what's someone else's to them. Boundaries are used to protect relationships, not hamper them. When you fail to establish or maintain boundaries by speaking your truth in all situations, you risk breaching your integrity. Let's see if you're maintaining your boundaries.

What are your crucial relationship boundaries? Is there someone who is always overstepping those boundaries? How do you deal with the breaches?

When, or with whom, do you tend to do what someone else wants rather than what you want?

_____

_____

_____

_____

_____

_____

_____

_____

_____

Who disapproves of your words or actions or tends to make you feel rejected? When they overstep your boundaries, do you call them out?

_____

_____

_____

_____

_____

_____

_____

_____

_____

_____

What have you been doing that doesn't feel right?

_____

_____

_____

_____

_____

_____

_____

_____

What do you regret doing and why?

_____

_____

_____

_____

_____

_____

_____

_____

"Being honest may not get you a lot of friends
but it'll always get you the right ones."

—JOHN LENNON

What does someone do that feels hurtful? How do you address it?

When do you tend to feel disrespected? Do you speak up?

Write what you would tell someone vital to your happiness when they offended you by disrespecting one of your "thou shalt nots."

_____

_____

_____

_____

_____

_____

_____

_____

_____

_____

_____

_____

_____

_____

_____

_____

_____

"Be impeccable with your word. Speak with integrity. Say only what you mean. Avoid using the word to speak against yourself or to gossip about others. Use the power of your word in the direction of truth and love."

—DON MIGUEL RUIZ, *THE FOUR AGREEMENTS: A PRACTICAL GUIDE TO PERSONAL FREEDOM*

Practice the Three Forms of Integrity

According to executive coach Dan Coughlin, there are three types of integrity:

1. **Internal integrity** *represents honoring your deepest core values—what you would choose to do in secret, even if you'd never be acknowledged or possibly earn respect for your actions. You sketched out your core values previously. Are you abiding by them?*

2. **External integrity** *is how you are in the wider world. How you speak and act with others, what you allow others to see. If there's disparity between what you believe and how you behave, you lack external integrity and need to work on truly speaking and acting in congruence with your deepest core values.*

3. **Image integrity** *is the true image of your integrity. This is you fully integrated, someone who is upfront, honest, and so clear that your actions or words cannot be misconstrued. This is not someone who presents false fronts on social media or pretends to be someone they are not.*

Ideally, you achieve internal and external integrity in order to make image integrity easy to achieve. Answer the following questions to see how you're doing.

Are you faithful to your deepest core values? If not, which ones are hardest to follow?

_____

_____

_____

_____

_____

_____

_____

_____

Where are you consistently falling short? What can you do to faithfully honor your deepest core values?

_____

_____

_____

_____

_____

_____

_____

_____

_____

Are you saying what you think and feel in every situation? Where does it feel unsafe to be you? What are you willing to do to change it?

_____

_____

_____

_____

_____

_____

_____

_____

What aspects of yourself still feel risky to reveal? What are you afraid would happen? Can you imagine a different outcome?

_____

_____

_____

_____

_____

_____

_____

_____

Do you stand up for your core beliefs? Are you willing to risk rejection over a belief you strongly hold?

_____

_____

_____

_____

_____

_____

_____

_____

Are you willing to risk relationships when a core value is absent or disrespected? Is there anyone in your life who creates situations you tolerate but don't address? How could you address them?

_____

_____

_____

_____

_____

_____

_____

_____

_____

Do you ever lie—to others or yourself? If so, what about and why? What would happen if you told the truth?

_____

_____

_____

_____

_____

_____

_____

_____

Do you put on any false pretenses? What are you afraid would happen if you were totally yourself in all situations?

_____

_____

_____

_____

_____

_____

_____

_____

_____

Have You Achieved Internal, External, and Image Integrity?

This is where the rubber meets the road. Time to take stock of how well you're doing living a life of integrity by working your way through the following questions.

When it comes to your profession, are you doing what you want? If not, why? What would you need to do to feel happy? What would be your ideal job? What would make it ideal? Brainstorm ideas for achieving integrity at work.

_____

_____

_____

_____

_____

_____

_____

_____

_____

_____

_____

_____

Do you have a five-year plan for what you want to achieve in life? Write down your five most important life goals and be as specific as possible. These should be based on your core values and your quest to live an authentic life.

1. _____

2. _____

3. _____

4. _____

5. _____

Do you have a ten-year plan for what you want to achieve in life? Write down the five most important goals, being as specific as possible.

1. _____

2. _____

3. _____

4. _____

5. _____

Are you in a successful, mutually fulfilling relationship? Do you feel and express what you think and feel with your partner? Your children? Do you regularly foster intimacy? What needs improvement?

_____

_____

_____

_____

_____

_____

_____

_____

_____

_____

Are you close to your extended family? Are they a priority? Do you often have intimate conversations with them? If you disagree strongly with family, do you speak up? What would it take to bolster your integrity here?

_____

_____

_____

_____

_____

_____

_____

_____

_____

How often do you see your closest friends? Are you your *authentic* self with your friends? What issues would you like to talk about with your friends that you haven't? Is there anyone you need to jettison?

_____

_____

_____

_____

_____

_____

_____

_____

_____

_____

_____

Outside of work, do you choose activities that reinforce your authentic self? List five ways you can do things that nurture the *you* in you.

1. _____

2. _____

3. _____

4. _____

5. _____

Do you have spiritual practice? Do you practice meditation or mindfulness? If not, how do you stay in touch with and honor your innermost self or soul?

_____

_____

_____

_____

_____

_____

_____

_____

_____

Do you make time to be alone? What do you most like to do when alone? What could you do to honor or express your *authentic* self when alone?

_____

_____

_____

_____

_____

_____

_____

_____

_____

Do you share your genuine self with others? Give back to your community or volunteer your time? If not, list three ways you can start doing so.

1. _____

2. _____ .

3. _____

ALWAYS ASSESS YOUR MOTIVATION

Your authentic self is frequently bombarded by internal motivations and external influences.

Internal motivators are those drives and desires that originate deep within and drive you to become a better person and pursue *your* values-based goals.

External motivators are decisions you make based on external factors like money, status, recognition, or other people's expectations.

To determine whether internal or external motivators are influencing your decisions, you can ask yourself:

· Do I feel pressured by other people into taking this step? If so, by whom?

· What do I want to accomplish with this goal?

· Am I willing to fight through difficult obstacles to make this happen?

· Is this truly what I want?

Remember to always listen carefully to what your logical, thinking brain says, but also consult your heart (feelings) and your gut instincts or reactions. Together, these senses comprise your intuition, where you may already know the answer deep down.

Do you make personal growth a priority? List five things you'd like to learn. Pick things that would bolster authenticity.

1. _____

2. _____

3. _____

4. _____

5. _____

How could you be more conscious and accountable to your ideals, or to something outside of yourself? For example, if protecting the earth is a major value, are you conserving resources and promoting recycling at home and work? List five ways you can be closer to your ideals.

1. _____

2. _____

3. _____

4. _____

5. _____

Now that you've mastered the integrity required to live an authentic life, let's discuss the essential, often challenging, task of finding your authentic life purpose.

CHAPTER SIX

FIND YOUR LIFE PURPOSE

To live an authentic life you need to have a sense of purpose, a reason for being that guides your choices in life—your reason for waking up in the morning. Otherwise, you could waste valuable time or end up feeling like an imposter and have massive regrets when your time runs out. All the work you've done up to now was designed to help you learn more about yourself, what's vital to your happiness, and to circle in closer to finding your life purpose. To get even closer to an answer, let's find out more about who you *really* are.

"Without a clear sense of purpose, it's easy to get sidetracked on your journey through life. Some people spend their whole lives aimlessly going off in all directions because they have no guiding principle pointing them toward a life that will truly make them happy."

—JACK CANFIELD

Do You Know Your Passions?

Whatever you're passionate about is a huge clue to what might be your life purpose. Passion signifies interest and investment. When you passionately care about something, it tells you rather a lot about who you might be under the hood.

What did you *love* to do as a child? What obsessed you as a teenager? A young adult? What aspect of those activities most fascinated or drove you to keep doing them?

_____

_____

_____

_____

_____

_____

_____

_____

> "Whatever it is, don't just look at the activities that keep you up all night but look at the cognitive principles behind those activities that enthrall you. Because they can easily be applied elsewhere."
>
> —MARK MANSON

Did people tease you—or envy you—over some ability or gift that seemed unique to you? What might they have secretly envied?

_____

_____

_____

_____

_____

Is there some activity that has always been an essential part of your life, something you can't live happily without doing?

_____

_____

_____

_____

_____

What were (are) you doing when you felt (feel) most like yourself? Take a moment to write about it and feel how it brings light into your life.

_____

_____

_____

_____

_____

What were (are) your secret pleasures? Is there something about you that you know is special but don't tell others?

_____

_____

_____

_____

_____

What do you do that energizes you or makes you feel joyous or celebratory when you complete it? Why does this activity bring such pleasure?

_____

_____

_____

_____

_____

Was there something you feared surrendering when you grew up, got a job, or got married?

_____

_____

_____

_____

_____

_____

What would you willingly endure sacrifice to do?

_____

_____

_____

_____

What have you done that filled you with pride?

_____

_____

_____

_____

If you had to choose three attributes about yourself that were all you could keep, what would they be?

1. _____

2. _____

3. _____

If someone told you that you could do whatever you wanted and earn a huge paycheck, what would you do?

_____

_____

_____

_____

If you could do *anything* to save the world, what would it be?

_____

_____

_____

_____

_____

_____

What would you do that would be worth dying for?

_____

_____

_____

_____

_____

_____

And again: If you knew you would die within a year, beyond being with
your loved ones, how would you spend your precious time?

_____

_____

_____

_____

_____

_____

Do You Know Your Soul?

Our soul is that part of us that loves passionately. It's the very core of who we are, something we often hide, or easily lose sight of, as we grow up. Think deeply and then answer the following questions. Meditate on *why* you chose each answer, because *why* matters most of all. If you don't know the answers, spend time figuring them out. This is how you reacquaint your exterior self with your deepest, authentic *self*.

My favorite artist is	

because...

My favorite work of art is	

because...

My favorite poet is	

because...

My favorite poem is

because...

_____

_____

_____

My favorite stage play is

because...

_____

_____

_____

My favorite novel is

because...

_____

_____

_____

My favorite character in a play, novel, or movie is

because...

_____

_____

_____

My favorite comedian, magician, or trickster is

because...

My favorite myth or fairy tale is

because...

My preferred spiritual practice is

because...

My true hero is

because...

If I could be anyone, I would be

because...

If my soul were an animal, it would be

because...

"When you have discovered what you can offer to others, when you feel that you are on your unique path, when you have an ongoing, honest, reliable connection to your inner wisdom, then you have found your unique spot in this world with all its craziness, sorrow, and joy. This discovery gives tremendous ease. You finally have a way of relating to work, lovers, friends, and spiritual practices with open-heartedness and intelligence. Problems, no matter how intense, are workable."

—SUSAN PIVER, *THE 100 HARD QUESTIONS FOR AN AUTHENTIC LIFE*

My favorite word is

because...

My ultimate guiding principle is

because...

Reading poetry, meditating or praying, communing with nature, listening to music, studying philosophy or the arts, and contributing to your community are all ways to deepen soul attachment. Make time regularly to honor your soul, and it will enrich your life—and bolster authenticity.

"When you live life connected to purpose, you don't have to chase opportunities, they come to you."

—SUE FITZMAURICE

WHY KNOWING YOUR LIFE PURPOSE MATTERS

Figuring out your life purpose isn't an esoteric pursuit; it has real consequences:

It keeps you clear and focused. You've cleared away the detritus to focus on what matters most, making it easier to prioritize and make decisions that move you closer to your ultimate life goals.

It fuels your goals. Once you're doing what you really want to do, your energy soars.

It reinforces core values. If you're doing work that's important to you and helping to create the kind of reality you want to live in, you're reinforcing your values daily.

It bolsters self-esteem. You are being true to yourself, living with integrity, which helps you see yourself in a positive light.

It encourages trust. When you are doing what your heart compels you to do, people trust your motivations. They'll help you bring your vision to life.

It creates gratitude. There's nothing like the happiness and fulfillment that comes from being able to focus on what truly matters to you and making a positive impact.

Knowing your life purpose brings meaning and clarity to choices as to how you spend your valuable time and live an authentic life.

Who Most Inspires You with Their Work or Good Deeds?

Beyond role models for a certain profession, think long and hard about who most inspires you—and why. It can be a former teacher or a world leader, someone who lives a small life, or someone who devotes themselves to others on a global stage. Choose someone who confidently and intentionally lives life to the beat of their own drum, with fearlessness and thoughtfulness. Choose someone whose guiding principles, dedication, integrity, activism, and achievement make you proud to be human. Would you cry if you saw them receive a major award? Why?

List five people and then note what has made the greatest impression on you.

1.

2.

3.

4.

5.

Write about what you think motivates these people to do what they do, be who they are, live with such authenticity.

_____

_____

_____

_____

List five ways you can replicate at least some of their practices and incorporate them into your daily life.

1. _____

2. _____

3. _____

4. _____

5. _____

FIND YOUR PURPOSE AND LIVE LONGER

A study of 7,000 older adults on the relationship between mortality and finding their life purpose found that those participants who lacked a strong sense of meaning in their lives were more than twice as likely to die prematurely as those who had found their purpose in life. Having a sense of purpose also reduced the incidence of cardiovascular events like heart attack and stroke. It's also essential for happiness and fulfillment.

Steps to Achieve Your Life Purpose

Once you've identified your life purpose, achieving it requires behavioral changes. Below is a list of changes that may be required. Circle or highlight those that you need to address.

- *Embrace simplicity.*
- *Allow for revision.*
- *Forgive mistakes—yours and others'.*
- *Be open to new experiences, new activities, and new thoughts.*
- *Do not compare your journey with anyone else's.*
- *Adjust your goals and expectations based on your priorities.*
- *Establish clearly defined boundaries, both with yourself and with others in your life.*
- *Schedule a regular time for self-reflection and self-evaluation.*
- *Stop chasing perfection.*

Of the steps you circled above, which ones need immediate attention, and how can you address them? Write about where you are falling short and your solutions.

_____

_____

_____

_____

_____

What's Your Future Story?

Many believe we consciously—or unconsciously—create a lot of our future. If you could create yours, what would it be? Think in broad strokes, or, if it seems more manageable, think only about the next five years as you ponder the following:

- *Who will be in it?*
- *What will you be doing?*
- *Where will you be?*
- *What will provide the most sense of fulfillment?*
- *What will be making you happy?*

Now spend ten minutes imagining your ideal life in which you will do what adds deep meaning to your life and brings you the greatest joy. Write a sketch of that life in terms of the above questions and anything else you can think of to flesh it out.

_____

_____

_____

_____

_____

_____

Use this as a visualization tool by printing your answer and posting it somewhere you can see it often.

What Is *Your* Life Purpose?

Now that we've gone through these exercises, it's time to pinpoint and then clearly state what your *authentic* self's life purpose is. Remember, abiding by this purpose and using it to motivate your choices and determine your actions is what will bring you the most joy, fulfillment, and energy. It's what you're willing to sacrifice time, money, and even family life to achieve. It's what you'd want highlighted in your obituary, what you want your true legacy to be.

Sample Life Purpose Declarations:

- *To inspire my own and others' children to know their own worth, develop faith in their ability, and learn to maximize their brainpower and passion in fulfilling whatever passions they hold.*
- *To inspire those around me to choose something beyond consumerism, promote the seeking and implementing of solutions for local preservation, and put this conviction into actionable works.*
- *To put my family first and foremost, to raise conscious, responsible, and caring children who will carry on our legacy.*
- *As a teacher, to inspire passion as well as trailblazing and independent thought so future generations will exceed our expectations.*

Now, write yours and be as specific as possible.

Create an Action Plan

Now that you know your life purpose, it's time to think about how you'll now live an authentic life, based on it and self-knowledge.

What in your current life is not creating or supporting your life purpose?

_____

_____

_____

_____

_____

_____

_____

What do you need to do to support your life purpose?

_____

_____

_____

_____

_____

_____

_____

List five things you can do to focus more on fulfilling your life purpose.

1.

2.

3.

4.

5.

What can you jettison to make more time for the goals of your life purpose?

Identifying your life purpose—though it's always open to revision—is a monumental task out of the way. Now that you have a clear life purpose, you can create concrete goals and action plans to work towards making this your guiding light. In doing so, you'll be taking a huge step toward authenticity. Please remember, however, that it's all an awakening process, one that can take years to fully develop and manifest. Let's close by discussing ways to make sure you're living an authentic life.

CHAPTER SEVEN

LIVE AN AUTHENTIC, MEANINGFUL LIFE

Once you have reconnected with your authentic self and fully committed to your life purpose, living a deep, meaningful life becomes possible. However, given all the stresses that will continue to challenge your focus, it's easy to slip backwards, lapse into the kind of unconscious functioning that drains away all the pleasures living your life purpose brings. This chapter will offer ways to keep your body, mind, and spirit focused on what matters most to you.

"We are not here to fit in, be well balanced, or provide exampla for others. We are here to be eccentric, different, perhaps strange, perhaps merely to add our small piece, our little clunky, chunky selves, to the great mosaic of being. As the gods intended, we are here to become more and more ourselves."

—JAMES HOLLIS, *WHAT MATTERS MOST: LIVING A MORE CONSIDERED LIFE*

Write in a Journal

To hyperfocus your mind/body/spirit on what matters most, spend five minutes a night writing down what happened each day and how it impacted you. This trains your brain to notice everything that is either supporting or thwarting your efforts to live an authentic life and fulfill your life purpose, which helps you take full responsibility on a daily basis. Try it here—then buy yourself a journal!

Write a journal entry below about your day. Focus on what most caught your attention—good, bad, or otherwise—and note what made you feel most alive, authentic, fulfilled. Make this a habit.

_____

_____

_____

_____

_____

_____

READ EVERY DAY

Challenge and stimulate your brain by spending at least thirty minutes a day reading or listening to something _substantive_. Read books about science, philosophy, psychology, history, and other topics you rarely explore. Biographies or historical and literary novels that explore something beyond surface concerns also count. Feed your brain something it can mull over, thereby stimulating ongoing thought and reflection. It also helps you clarify your values and discover new interests.

Stay Fully Awake

Now that you've worked so hard to achieve consciousness, here's an effortless way to recognize when you're awake and alive, focused on living authentically and pursuing your life purpose, or in danger of falling back to sleep and losing sight of what most matters to your true happiness.

When Unconscious, You Feel:	When Fully Awake/Conscious, You Feel:
Asleep at the wheel	Awake, lucid, aware
Gripped by emotions	Mindfully observing emotions
Disassociated	Experiencing feelings
Heart closed, defensive	Heart open, loving
Reactive	Responsive
Grasping, resisting	Balanced, discerning

If you're struggling, use the many tools we've discussed—meditation, mindfulness, tuning in to your feelings, managing your emotions, reviewing your values, and so on—to refocus your body/mind/spirit on your life purpose and what matters most.

You might want to create your own list of symptoms, what happens when *you* are not focused on being authentic or living your life purpose, and post it on your refrigerator or bathroom mirror. Also post the positives list, and every time you read how well you're doing, take a moment to honor your focus, your intentions, and your commitment to being your authentic self.

How do you know when you're not living authentically?

_____

_____

_____

_____

_____

_____

How do you know when you're being fully authentic and pursuing your life purpose?

_____

_____

_____

_____

_____

_____

"Authenticity is about being true to who
you are, even when everyone around
you wants you to be someone else."

—MICHAEL JORDAN

Record Your Dreams

Even if you don't understand what the symbols mean, recording your dreams honors the work your subconscious does to make sense of your world or to communicate what's worrying your authentic self. Over time, you will gain insight into what your symbols mean—or at least you'll begin to see patterns and understand what troubles your subconscious.

Have you noticed any recurring symbols in your dreams?

_____

_____

_____

Are you aware of issues that reoccur in your dreams?

_____

_____

_____

If someone is constantly showing up in your dreams, what do you think they want you to know?

_____

_____

_____

Count Your Blessings

Feeling and expressing *genuine* gratitude for all the good in your life fosters happiness—and increased blessings. It trains your brain to focus on all the good that happens and teaches you to appreciate your good fortune. This helps you feel safe, grounded, and empowered, which bolsters your ability to live authentically.

Starting today, list ten things in your life for which you are exceedingly grateful:

1. _____

2. _____

3. _____

4. _____

5. _____

6. _____

7. _____

8. _____

9. _____

10. _____

It's a great idea to write down what you feel grateful for on a regular basis. This not only bolsters happiness in general, but it can help you stay focused on what matters—what contributes to living your authentic life.

Address Concerns as They Arise

One of the best ways to honor your *authentic* self is to know what's going on with you, moment to moment. Use the following RAIN acronym—originally developed by Buddhist teacher Michele McDonald—as a tool for untangling emotional suffering and living in conscious presence, by awakening mindfulness and compassion and applying them to the places where you get stuck.

Recognize: Ask yourself, "What is happening inside me, right now?" See it, feel it, name it.

Allow: Ask yourself, "Can I be with this?" Or "Can I let this be?" *Let it be*, focus on your breath, slowly breathe in and out until calm. Use this method as an alternative to anger, reactivity, anxiety, worry, defensiveness, addictive behavior, and self-blame.

Investigate with gentle curiosity. "What caught my attention? What am I feeling? How strong is the feeling in my body? Does it feel appropriate, overly reactive? Does it remind my body of past experiences? What feels essential to my most vulnerable self to express?" Don't think about this; try instead to "sense" the answers in your body.

Nurture with lovingkindness. Acknowledge your wounded soul and offer yourself nurturance: a hand over your heart, take a deep breath, offer yourself compassion, kindness, understanding.

Try this check-in exercise. Think of a situation that is causing you distress.

Recognize:
_____
_____
_____

Allow:
_____
_____
_____

Investigate:
_____
_____
_____

Nurture:
_____
_____
_____

Use this check-in method whenever you feel off course or need to refocus your energy on what matters most.

"If you find yourself criticizing other people, you're probably doing it out of *Resistance*. When we see others beginning to live their authentic selves, it drives us crazy if we have not lived out our own. Individuals who are realized in their own lives almost never criticize others. If they speak at all, it is to offer encouragement. Watch yourself. Of all the manifestations of *Resistance*, most only harm ourselves. Criticism and cruelty harm others as well."

—STEVEN PRESSFIELD, *THE WAR OF ART: BREAK THROUGH THE BLOCKS AND WIN YOUR INNER CREATIVE BATTLES*

Keep Your Brain Bathed in Happiness

To live an authentic life, making sure your brain is regularly stimulated in ways that bolster happiness is essential. Here're the four essential happiness chemicals in the brain and activities you can do to stimulate them.

Dopamine, **the Reward Chemical**	Eat nutritious food.
	Achieve a goal.
	Complete a task.
	Practice self-care.

Endorphin, **the Painkilling Chemical**	Exercise vigorously.
	Listen to music.
	Watch a happy movie.
	Laugh.

Serotonin, **the Mood Chemical**	Sit in the sun.
	Practice mindfulness.
	Be with nature.
	Meditate.

	Socialize.
Oxytocin, **the Love Chemical**	Touch and be touched.
	Pet an animal.
	Help others.

TRY SLEEP THINKING PROMPTS

To find answers about your inner self, Eric Maisel, a writer and creativity coach, suggests *sleep thinking prompts*. Pose a question to your brain prior to sleep and see what your lovely brain delivers in the morning. Three questions—one per night—to ask could be: What do I need more of in my life? What do I need to stop obsessing about? What could be next for me?

> "If you suddenly and unexpectedly feel joy, don't hesitate. Give in to it."
>
> —MARY OLIVER, *DEVOTIONS*

Be Curious about Your Life

As you go through your day, pause to simply notice what you are choosing to do, say, or think, and then—gently—ask yourself *why* you are making those choices. This is not meant to be judgmental or to feel interrogational, which isn't productive. It's simply another way to notice what you truly value. Consider it being curious about yourself. This encourages and reinforces future engagement.

What captured your attention today?

_____

_____

_____

_____

_____

What did you think about it?

_____

_____

_____

_____

_____

_____

_____

What got shuffled to the side?

_____

_____

_____

_____

_____

_____

How do you feel about your choices?

_____

_____

_____

_____

_____

DO SOMETHING!

Often when we feel dejected, it's because our choices are not honoring our core values. If you love nurturing the planet, for example, recognizing and honoring that value will help make life feel authentic and purposeful. Perhaps take classes on gardening, join a gardening club and share your passion, or volunteer to help plant a local garden. Choose activities that support and honor your underlying value and you'll soon feel cheerful and upbeat.

Learn Something You Always Wanted to Learn

In a Dallas Lifespan Brain Study, a group of older adults met just to socialize, while another group met to learn something new together like digital photography or quilting. The ones who met to learn a new skill had larger improvements in a variety of cognitive areas, from episodic memory to processing speed. Learning with other people seemed to light up their brains, particularly when they could learn at their own pace and not be or feel judged.

Lifelong learning expands who you are and how you think. Making time to learn something that fascinates you honors your authentic self. Besides, how do you know who you are and what you genuinely like if you aren't exploring new activities?

What is something that has always fascinated you that you haven't pursued?

_____

_____

_____

What kinds of things would you like to learn or explore?

_____

_____

_____

_____

Why haven't you found a way to do it? What can you do to pursue learning?

_____

_____

_____

_____

_____

_____

EMBRACE THE PRINCIPLES OF LEARNING

Here's what we know about learning:

1. We all have latent abilities waiting to be stimulated.
2. Developing skills takes time—and practice.
3. Failure is an essential part of learning.
4. Varying the skills you practice benefits learning.
5. Your progress may not be linear; you may get worse before you get better.
6. Skills rarely transfer.
7. You have to push the limits, stretch beyond your comfort zone.
8. Learning new skills opens up new worlds.

Embrace the principles of learning and open yourself up to new possibilities.

Offer Yourself Love

One of the best ways to honor your *innermost* self is to treat yourself like you'd treat someone you love. Extending small kindness on a regular basis would be one way to show love. Pampering is another. Fulfilling needs and wants, sharing generously, honoring and respecting are all ways we can show love to others and to ourselves. Give yourself daily credit for living an authentic life. Meanwhile, let's see how you're doing on loving yourself.

How often do you focus on your *self* and *your* needs?

_____

_____

_____

_____

_____

When was the last time you did something special just for you? What was it? How did it feel to focus solely on yourself and fulfill a desire or want?

_____

_____

_____

_____

_____

_____

Are you aware of something you need or want to do that you haven't done?
If not, why? Can you do it now? How would it feel to honor that need?

_____

_____

_____

_____

_____

_____

_____

_____

_____

Is there something left unsaid that needs to be said? Can you write about it
here, then say it?

_____

_____

_____

_____

_____

_____

_____

_____

_____

_____

Is there an issue that you've not addressed with someone? Can you write about it, then address it with said person?

_____

_____

_____

_____

_____

How would you like someone else to show love to you? Have you told the person what you want? If not, why?

_____

_____

_____

_____

_____

_____

Is this something you can do for yourself? Why haven't you done so?

_____

_____

_____

_____

_____

Practice Self-Love

Check in regularly to make sure you're offering yourself the depth of love you'd offer to someone you treasure. Are you offering yourself:

Awareness?	YES	NO
Lovingkindness?	YES	NO
Emotional comfort?	YES	NO
Respect?	YES	NO
Appreciation for small favors?	YES	NO
Daily encouragement?	YES	NO
Attentive listening?	YES	NO
Physical pampering?	YES	NO

Write about any areas where you're falling short and then make efforts to do better. Remember, this kind of attentiveness to *self* reinforces your ability to live more authentically.

_____

_____

_____

_____

_____

_____

Embrace Enchantment

The more you notice the small natural and surprising wonders occurring all around you, the more you train your consciousness to see and appreciate them in the moment. Feeling enchanted helps you remember that life is precious and filled with small miracles. It also helps you feel the *joy* that comes with living an authentic life. Here are ways you can invite enchantment into your life:

- *Spend a day in nature photographing beauty, from large vistas to micro stems.*
- *Search until you find a poem that takes your breath away.*
- *Listen to a violin concerto or your favorite operatic solo.*
- *Hike through the woods and silently observe a waterfall.*
- *Light candles and sit in absolute silence.*

START SMALL

When recognizing joyful feelings, start small. Jump in a mud puddle and notice the childlike joy that washes over you. Linger in a hug and feel the love someone is offering. Taste something delicious and savor the pleasure it brings. Connecting conscious observance to small feelings helps you learn to feel everything more fully.

Be in Nature

There's no better way to quiet the overstimulation modern life brings than to turn your cell phone off and venture into nature. Sans agenda, make time in your life to simply "be" yourself outdoors. While there, notice all the marvelous sights, sounds, smells, and tastes nature has to offer. Drink them in, savor them, and write about them later. This type of mindful silence reinforces your ability to access your authentic self, separate from daily demands.

ASK THESE 3 QUESTIONS OFTEN

At least once a week, ask yourself the following questions:

- What has my body made clear it needs or wants that I've not given it?
- What has my mind desired that I've somehow ignored?
- What does my spirit want from me that I failed to give it?

This kind of mindfulness towards *self* helps you live more authentically.

"Those who contemplate the beauty of the earth find reserves of strength that will endure as long as life lasts."

— RACHEL CARSON, *THE SENSE OF WONDER*

Delight in Being Alone

You don't have to wait until you have a partner or friend to join you in activities, particularly when those activities reflect and delight your authentic self. If there's something you love doing, something that makes you feel like you, why not do it alone? Do you love art galleries or craft fairs? Do you love hiking? Do you love sad movies? Do you love sailing?

List five activities you love to do—usually with others—but are open to exploring solo.

1.
2.
3.
4.
5.

What have you dreamed about doing but haven't yet tried? (Hint: List it, then do it!)

1.
2.
3.
4.
5.

What feeds your soul? Do these activities often.

1. _____
2. _____
3. _____
4. _____
5. _____

What do you hate doing? Can you hire someone else to do it, or at least transform the way you look at the task?

1. _____
2. _____
3. _____
4. _____
5. _____

When you're alone, what brings you pleasure? Listening to music? Dancing naked? Taking a hot bath? List five things you can do to not only enjoy but thrill in being alone.

1. _____
2. _____
3. _____
4. _____
5. _____

List any objects you love and why—how they reflect your *authentic* self. Are they incorporated into your living space?

1. _____

2. _____

3. _____

4. _____

5. _____

BE A DAY-TRIPPER

To reinforce your authentic self, select one day a month when you can do *you*—just you. Preferably make it a day trip somewhere, perhaps alone, doing something that brings *you* massive pleasure. Spend the time being fully conscious of how much pleasure you're experiencing. Take photos, and journal about your day later.

Where Are You Now?

We started with a quiz to see where you were with living authentically, so here's another quiz to see how far you've come in manifesting and reinforcing your *authentic* self. Answer yes or no and then write about any areas that need additional attention.

Are you more concerned with truth than opinions?	YES	NO
When you express your feelings, are you sincere and not given to pretense?	YES	NO
Are you living life free from hypocrisy, or "walking your talk," in all areas of your life?	YES	NO
Do you know who your authentic self is and constantly strive to be that person?	YES	NO
Are you comfortable allowing others to see your vulnerabilities?	YES	NO
Do you feel more confident in who your *authentic* self is now?	YES	NO
Are there still places in your life where you suppress your authentic self?	YES	NO
Have you identified and maintained personal boundaries?	YES	NO
Do you walk away from situations where you can't be yourself?	YES	NO
Do you often act in ways that you feel are required to make you likable?	YES	NO
Do you feel awake to your own feelings?	YES	NO

Are you able to manage yours and others' difficult or hard emotions?	YES	NO
When others share difficult emotions, are you a good listener?	YES	NO
Are you free from others' opinions of you?	YES	NO
Have you become more compassionate towards yourself and others?	YES	NO
Are you more open and self-revealing with your family and friends?	YES	NO
Are you more accepting and loving of yourself?	YES	NO
Are you in a job that suits your authentic self?	YES	NO
Are you making time for activities that reinforce and express your authentic self?	YES	NO
Do you regularly tend to your soul?	YES	NO

Now write about anything that stood out from the quiz. Where do you still have work to do?

_____

_____

_____

_____

_____

_____

_____

Congratulations! Throughout this process, you've learned a lot about your*self*. Use this space to further validate what you've learned about your essential, authentic self—those parts of you that come naturally, who you are when you most feel like *you*, any gifts or proclivities you may have that make you stand out from others. Record what makes you *you* here.

_____

_____

_____

_____

_____

_____

_____

_____

_____

_____

Now that you know who you are, go out there and be fully you with all the satisfaction, enrichment, and joy that living authentically brings.

"Never apologize for burning too brightly, or for collapsing into yourself every night. That is how galaxies are made."
—TYLER KENT WHITE, *SONGS WITH OUR EYES CLOSED*

Quarto

This edition published in 2023 by Chartwell Books,
an imprint of The Quarto Group
142 West 36th Street, 4th Floor
New York, NY 10018 USA
T (212) 779-4972 F (212) 779-6058
www.Quarto.com

10 9 8 7 6 5 4 3 2 1

Chartwell titles are also available at discount for retail, wholesale, promotional, and bulk purchase. For details, contact the Special Sales Manager by email at specialsales@quarto.com or by mail at The Quarto Group, Attn: Special Sales Manager, 100 Cummings Center Suite 265D, Beverly, MA 01915, USA.

ISBN: 978-0-7858-4347-4

Publisher: Wendy Friedman
Senior Publishing Manager: Meredith Mennitt
Senior Design Manager: Michael Caputo
Editor: Jennifer Kushnier
Designer: Kate Sinclair

All stock photos and design elements ©Shutterstock

Printed in China

This book provides general information. It should not be relied upon as recommending or promoting any specific diagnosis or method of treatment for a particular condition. It is not intended as a substitute for medical advice or for direct diagnosis and treatment of a medical or psychological condition by a qualified physician or therapist. Readers who have questions about a particular condition, possible treatments for that condition, or possible reactions from the condition or its treatment should consult a physician, therapist, or other qualified healthcare professional.